THE ALPINE PATH

Green Gables Edition

PRODUCED EXCLUSIVELY FOR THE
BOUTIQUE GREEN GABLES GIFT SHOP

THE
ALPINE PATH

THE STORY OF MY CAREER

by

L. M. MONTGOMERY

Green Gables Edition

This book was purchased at the
BOUTIQUE GREEN GABLES GIFT SHOP
located at Green Gables Site, Prince Edward Island National Park,
Cavendish, Prince Edward Island, Canada.

Nimbus Publishing Limited
PO Box 9166, Halifax, NS   B3K 5M8
(902) 455-4286

Printed and bound in Canada

Published with the kind permission of Dr. Stuart Macdonald. The publishers gratefully acknowledge the help of Mrs. Donald St. John.

Interior Design: Terri Strickland
Cover: Kathy Kaulbach, Paragon Design

Library and Archives Canada Cataloguing in Publication

Montgomery, L. M. (Lucy Maud), 1874-1942.
The alpine path : the story of my career / L. M. Montgomery.
Originally published in 6 installments in Everywomen's world, 1917.
ISBN 1-55109-532-7

1. Montgomery, L. M. (Lucy Maud), 1874-1942. 2. Novelists, Canadian (English)—20th century—Biography. I. Title. II. Title: Everywoman's world.

PS8526.O55Z46 2005   C813'.52   C2005-902967-6

We acknowledge the financial support of the Government of Canada through the Book Publishing Industry Development Program (BPIDP) and the Canada Council, and of the Province of Nova Scotia through the Department of Tourism, Culture and Heritage for our publishing activities.

❦ Preface ❧

IN 1917 THE editor of *Everywoman's World*, a magazine published in Toronto from 1911 until the 1920s, asked L.M.
Montgomery to write the story of her career. What she produced was published in six instalments, June through
November, under the title she chose, *The Alpine Path*. It came
from a verse that had been her inspiration during the long
years when success as a writer seemed remote and only dogged
determination kept her on

> The Alpine path, so hard, so steep,
> That leads to heights sublime.

Lucy Maud Montgomery was 42 in 1917, married to the
Reverend Ewan MacDonald and the mother of two small sons.
She had been writing professionally for over twenty years and
it was nearly ten years since the publication of *Anne of Green
Gables*, her first book, had made her world famous. In the
meantime she had published eight additional books including
several of the *Anne* series and also her own favourite, *The Story
Girl*. In the years that followed 1917 she published another fif-
teen books, among them several more of the *Anne* series, the
Emily books, and her two "adult" novels, *Magic for Marigold* and
The Blue Castle. Moreover she continued the freelance magazine
writing with which she had begun her career.

The Alpine Path is the most complete source of information about the childhood and early struggles of this accomplished and well-loved Canadian writer. She wrote it, she said, "to encourage some other toiler who is struggling along in the weary pathway I once followed to success." But in addition to describing her apprenticeship as a writer, L.M. Montgomery gives here a rich, idyllic description of her childhood in Prince Edward Island and of the sources of some people and places in her novels.

This edition of *The Alpine Path*, which is its first publication in any form since 1917, reproduces the complete text. New chapter breaks replace the original arbitrary instalment breaks. True to her own admission that she could never remember dates, Maud Montgomery forgot the year of her honeymoon. It was 1911, not 1912 as stated in the concluding section of the book.

THE ALPINE PATH

❦ Chapter One ❧

WHEN THE EDITOR of *Everywoman's World* asked me to write "The Story of My Career," I smiled with a little touch of incredulous amusement. My career? *Had* I a career? Was not—should not—a "career" be something splendid, wonderful, spectacular at the very least, something varied and exciting? Could my long, uphill struggle, through many quiet, uneventful years, be termed a "career"? It had never occurred to me to call it so; and, on first thought, it did not seem to me that there was much to be said about that same long, monotonous struggle. But it appeared to be a whim of the aforesaid editor that I should say what little there was to be said; and in those same long years I acquired the habit of accommodating myself to the whims of editors to such an inveterate degree that I have not yet been able to shake it off. So I shall cheerfully tell my tame story. If it does nothing else, it may serve to encourage some other toiler who is struggling along in the weary pathway I once followed to success.

Many years ago, when I was still a child, I clipped from a current magazine a bit of verse, entitled "To the Fringed Gentian," and pasted it on the corner of the little portfolio on which I wrote my letters and school essays. Every time I opened the portfolio I read one of those verses over; it was the key-note of my every aim and ambition:

"Then whisper, blossom, in thy sleep
   How I may upward climb
The Alpine path, so hard, so steep,
   That leads to heights sublime;
How I may reach that far-off goal
   Of true and honoured fame,
And write upon its shining scroll
   A woman's humble name."

It is indeed a "hard and steep" path; and if any word I can write will assist or encourage another pilgrim along that path, that word I gladly and willingly write.

I was born in the little village of Clifton, Prince Edward Island. "Old Prince Edward Island" is a good place in which to be born—a good place in which to spend a childhood. I can think of none better. We Prince Edward Islanders are a loyal race. In our secret soul we believe that there is no place like the little Province that gave us birth. We may suspect that it isn't *quite* perfect, any more than any other spot on this planet, but you will not catch us admitting it. And how furiously we hate anyone who does say it! The only way to inveigle a Prince Edward Islander into saying anything in dispraise of his beloved Province is to praise it extravagantly to him. Then, in order to deprecate the wrath of the gods and veil decently his own bursting pride, he will, perhaps, be induced to state that it has one or two drawbacks—mere spots on the sun. But his hearer must not commit the unpardonable sin of agreeing with him!

Prince Edward Island, however, is really a beautiful Province—the most beautiful place in America, I believe. Elsewhere are more lavish landscapes and grander scenery; but for chaste, restful loveliness it is unsurpassed. "Compassed by the inviolate sea," it floats on the waves of the blue gulf, a green seclusion and "haunt of ancient peace."

Much of the beauty of the Island is due to the vivid colour contrasts—the rich red of the winding roads, the brilliant emerald of the uplands and meadows, the glowing sapphire of the encircling sea. It is the sea which makes Prince Edward Island in more senses than the geographical. You cannot get away from the sea down there. Save for a few places in the interior, it is ever visible somewhere, if only in a tiny blue gap between distant hills, or a turquoise gleam through the dark boughs of spruce fringing an estuary. Great is our love for it; its tang gets into our blood: its siren call rings ever in our ears; and no matter where we wander in lands afar, the murmur of its waves ever summons us back in our dreams to the homeland. For few things am I more thankful than for the fact that I was born and bred beside that blue St. Lawrence Gulf.

And yet we cannot define the charm of Prince Edward Island in terms of land or sea. It is too elusive—too subtle. Sometimes I have thought it was the touch of austerity in an Island landscape that gives it its peculiar charm. And whence comes that austerity? Is it in the dark dappling of spruce and fir? Is it in the glimpses of sea and river? Is it in the bracing tang of the salt air? Or does it go deeper still, down to the very soul of the land? For lands have personalities just as well as human beings; and to know that personality you must live in the land and companion it, and draw sustenance of body and spirit from it; so only can you really know a land and be known of it.

My father was Hugh John Montgomery; my mother was Clara Woolner Macneill. So I come of Scotch ancestry, with a dash of English from several "grands" and "greats." There were many traditions and tales on both sides of the family, to which, as a child, I listened with delight while my elders talked them over around winter firesides. The romance of them was in my blood; I thrilled to the lure of adventure which had led my forefathers westward from the Old Land—a land which I always heard referred to as "Home," by men and women whose parents were Canadian born and bred.

Hugh Montgomery came to Canada from Scotland. He sailed on a vessel bound for Quebec; but the fates and a woman's will took a hand in the thing. His wife was desperately seasick all the way across the Atlantic—and a voyage over the Atlantic was no five days' run then. Off the north shore of Prince Edward Island, then a wild, wooded land, with settlements few and far between, the Captain hove-to in order to replenish his supply of water. He sent a boat ashore, and he told poor Mrs. Montgomery that she might go in it for a little change. Mrs. Montgomery did go in it; and when she felt that blessed dry land under her feet once more, she told her husband that she meant to stay there. Never again would she set foot in any vessel. Expostulation, entreaty, argument, all availed nothing. There the poor lady was resolved to stay, and there, perforce, her husband had to stay with her. So the Montgomerys came to Prince Edward Island.

Their son Donald, my great-grandfather, was the hero of another romance of those early days. I have used this tale in my book, *The Story Girl*. The Nancy and Betty Sherman of the story told there were Nancy and Betsy Penman, daughters of a United Empire Loyalist who came from the States at the close of the war of Independence. George Penman had been a paymaster in the British Army; having forfeited all his property, he was very poor, but the beauty of the Penman girls, especially Nancy, was so great that they had no lack of suitors from far and near. The Donald Fraser of *The Story Girl* was Donald Montgomery, and Neil Campbell was David Murray, of Bedeque. The only embroidery I permitted myself in the telling of the tale was to give Donald a horse and cutter. In reality, what he had was a half-broken steer, hitched to a rude, old wood-sled, and it was with this romantic equipage that he hied him over to Richmond Bay to propose to Nancy!

My grandfather, Senator Montgomery, was the son of Donald and Nancy, and inherited his stately presence and handsome face from his mother. He married his first cousin, Annie Murray, of Bedeque, the daughter of David and Betsy. So that Nancy and Betsy were both my great-grandmothers. If Betsy were alive today, I have no doubt she would be an ardent suffragette. The most advanced feminist could hardly spurn old conventions more effectually than she did when she proposed to David. I may add that I was always told that she and David were the happiest couple in the world.

It was from my mother's family—the Macneills—that I inherited my knack of writing and my literary tastes. John Macneill had come to Prince Edward Island in 1775; his family belonged to Argyleshire and had been adherents of the unfortunate Stuarts. Consequently, young Macneill found that a change of climate would probably be beneficial. Hector Macneill, a minor Scottish poet, was a cousin of his. He was the author of several beautiful and well-known lyrics, among them "Saw ye my wee thing, saw ye my ain thing," "I lo'e ne'er a laddie but one," and "Come under my plaidie"—the latter often and erroneously attributed to Burns.

John Macneill settled on a north-shore farm in Cavendish and had a family of twelve children, the oldest being William Macneill, my great-grandfather, commonly known as "Old Speaker Macneill." He was a very clever man, well educated for those times, and exercised a wide influence in provincial politics. He married Eliza Townsend, whose father was Captain John Townsend of the British Navy. His father, James Townsend, had received a grant of Prince Edward Island land from George III, which he called Park Corner, after the old family estate in England. Thither he came, bringing his wife. Bitterly homesick she was—rebelliously so. For weeks after her arrival she would not take off her bonnet, but walked the floor in it, imperiously demanding to be taken home. We children who heard the tale never wearied of speculating as to whether she took off her bonnet at night and put it on again in the morning, or whether she slept in it. But back home she could not go, so eventually she took off her bonnet and resigned herself to her fate. Very peacefully she sleeps in the little, old, family graveyard on the banks of the "Lake of Shining Waters"— in other words, Campbell's Pond at Park Corner. An old, red sandstone slab marks the spot where she and her husband lie, and on it is carved this moss-grown epitaph—one of the diffuse epitaphs of a generation that had time to carve such epitaphs and time to read them.

"To the memory of James Townsend, of Park Corner, Prince Edward Island. Also of Elizabeth, his wife. They emigrated from England to this Island, A.D. 1775, with two sons and three daughters, viz., John, James, Eliza, Rachel, and Mary. Their son John died in Antigua in the lifetime of his parents. His afflicted mother followed him into Eternity with patient resignation on the seventeenth day of April, 1795, in the 69th year of her age.

And her disconsolate husband departed this life on the 2 5th day of December, 1806, in the 87th year of his age."

I wonder if any homesick dreams haunt Elizabeth Townsend's slumber of over a hundred years!

William and Eliza Macneill had a large family of which all the members possessed marked intellectual power. Their education consisted only in the scanty, occasional terms of the district school of those rude, early days; but, had circumstances been kinder, some of them would have climbed high. My grandfather, Alexander Macneill, was a man of strong and pure literary tastes, with a considerable knack of prose composition. My great-uncle, William Macneill, could write excellent satirical verse. But his older brother, James Macneill, was a born poet. He composed hundreds of poems, which he would sometimes recite to favoured persons. They were never written down, and not a line of them, so far as I know, is now extant. But I heard my grandfather repeat many of them, and they were real poetry, most of them being satirical or mock-heroic. They were witty, pointed, and dramatic. Uncle James was something of a "mute, inglorious" Burns. Circumstances compelled him to spend his life on a remote Prince Edward Island farm; had he had the advantages of education that are within reach of any schoolboy to-day, I am convinced he would have been neither mute nor inglorious.

The "Aunt Mary Lawson," to whom I dedicated *The Story Girl*, was another daughter of William and Eliza Macneill. No story of my "career" would be complete without a tribute to her, for she was one of the formative influences of my childhood. She was really quite the most wonderful woman in many respects that I have ever known. She had never had any educational advantages. But she had a naturally powerful mind, a keen intelligence, and a most remarkable memory which retained to the day of her death all that she had ever heard or read or seen. She was a brilliant conversationalist, and it was a treat to get Aunt Mary started on tales and recollections of her youth, and all the vivid doings and sayings, of the folk in those young years of the Province. We were "chums," she and I, when she was in the seventies and I was in my teens. I cannot, in any words at my command, pay the debt I owe to Aunt Mary Lawson.

When I was twenty-one months old my mother died, in the old home at Cavendish, after a lingering illness. I distinctly remember seeing her in her coffin—it is my earliest memory. My father was standing by the casket holding me in his arms. I wore a little white dress of embroidered muslin, and Father was crying. Women were seated around the room, and I recall two in front of me on the sofa who were whispering to each other and looking pityingly at Father and me. Behind them the window was open, and green vines were trailing across it, while their shadows danced over the floor in a square of sunshine.

I looked down at Mother's dead face. It was a sweet face, albeit worn and wasted by months of suffering. My mother had been beautiful, and Death, so cruel in all else, had spared the delicate outline of feature, the long silken lashes brushing the hollow cheek, and the smooth masses of golden-brown hair.

I did not feel any sorrow, for I knew nothing of what it all meant. I was only vaguely troubled. Why was Mother so still? And why was Father crying? I reached down and laid my baby hand against Mother's cheek. Even yet I can feel the coldness of that touch. Somebody in the room sobbed and said, "Poor child." The chill of Mother's face had frightened me; I turned and put my arms appealingly about Father's neck and he kissed me. Comforted, I looked down again at the sweet, placid face as he carried me away. That one precious memory is all I have of the girlish mother who sleeps in the old burying-ground of Cavendish, lulled forever by the murmur of the sea.

❧ Chapter Two ❧

I WAS BROUGHT up by my grandparents in the old Macneill Homestead in Cavendish. Cavendish is a farming settlement on the north shore of Prince Edward Island. It was eleven miles from a railway and twenty-four miles from the nearest town. It was settled in 1700 by three Scotch families—the Macneills, Simpsons, and Clarks. These families had inter-married to such an extent that it was necessary to be born or bred in Cavendish in order to know whom it was safe to criticize. I heard Aunt Mary Lawson once naively admit that "the Macneills and Simpsons always considered themselves a little better than the common run;" and there was a certain rather ill-natured local saying which was always being cast up to us of the clans by outsiders, "From the conceit of the Simpsons, the pride of the Macneills, and the vain-glory of the Clarks, good Lord deliver us." Whatever were their faults, they were loyal, clannish, upright, God-fearing folk, inheriting traditions of faith and simplicity and aspiration.

I spent my childhood and girlhood in an old-fashioned Cavendish farmhouse, surrounded by apple orchards. The first six years of my life are hazy in recollection. Here and there, a memory picture stands out in vivid colours. One of these was the wonderful moment when, I fondly supposed, I discovered the exact locality of Heaven.

One Sunday, when I could not have been more than four years

old, I was in the old Clifton Church with Aunt Emily. I heard the minister say something about Heaven—that strange, mysterious place about which my only definite idea was that it was "where Mother had gone."

"Where is Heaven?" I whispered to Aunt Emily, although I knew well that whispering in church was an unpardonable sin. Aunt Emily did not commit it. Silently, gravely, she pointed upward. With the literal and implicit belief of childhood, I took it for granted that this meant that portion of Clifton Church which was above the ceiling. There was a little square hole in the ceiling. Why could we not go up through it and see Mother? This was a great puzzle to me. I resolved that when I grew bigger I would go to Clifton and find some means of getting up into Heaven and finding Mother. This belief and hope was a great, though secret, comfort to me for several years. Heaven was no remote, unattainable place—"some brilliant but distant shore." No, no! It was only ten miles away, in the attic of Clifton Church! Very, very sadly and slowly I surrendered that belief.

Hood wrote, in his charming *I Remember* that he was farther off from Heaven than when he was a boy. To me, too, the world seemed a colder, lonelier place when age and experience at length forced upon my reluctant seven-year-old consciousness the despairing conviction that Heaven was not so near me as I had dreamed. Mayhap, 'twas even nearer, "nearer than breathing, closer than hands or feet" but the ideas of childhood are, necessarily, very concrete; and when I once accepted the fact that the gates of pearl and streets of gold were not in the attic of Clifton Church, I felt as though they might as well be beyond the farthest star.

Many of those early memories are connected with visits to Grandfather Montgomery's farm at Park Corner. He and his

family lived in the "old house" then, a most quaint and delightful old place as I remember it, full of cupboards and nooks, and
little, unexpected flights of stairs. It was there, when I was
about five years old, that I had the only serious illness of my
life—an attack of typhoid fever.

The night before I took ill I was out in the kitchen with the
servants, feeling as well as usual, "wide-awake and full of gin-
ger," as the old cook used to declare. I was sitting before the
stove, and cook was "riddling" the fire with a long, straight bar
of iron used for that purpose. She laid it down on the hearth
and I promptly caught it up, intending to do some "riddling"
myself, an occupation I much liked, loving to see the glowing
red embers fall down on the black ashes.

Alas, I picked the poker up by the wrong end! As a result,
my hand was terribly burned. It was my first initiation into
physical pain, at least, the first one of which I have any
recollection.

I suffered horribly and cried bitterly; yet I took considerable
satisfaction out of the commotion I had caused. For the time
being I was splendidly, satisfyingly important. Grandfather
scolded the poor, distracted cook. Father entreated that something be done for me, frenzied folk ran about suggesting and
applying a score of different remedies. Finally I cried myself to
sleep, holding my hand and arm to the elbow in a pail of ice-cold
water, the only thing that gave me any relief.

I awoke next morning with a violent headache that grew
worse as the day advanced. In a few days the doctor pro-
nounced my illness to be typhoid fever. I do not know how
long I was ill, but several times I was very low and nobody
thought I could possibly recover.

Grandmother Macneill was sent for at the beginning of my illness. I was so delighted to see her that the excitement increased my fever to an alarming pitch, and after she had gone out, Father, thinking to calm me, told me that she had gone home. He meant well, but it was an unfortunate statement. I believed it implicitly—too implicitly. When Grandmother came in again I could not be convinced that it was she. No! She *had* gone home. Consequently, this woman must be Mrs. Murphy, a woman who worked at Grandfather's frequently, and who was tall and thin, like Grandmother.

I did not like Mrs. Murphy and I flatly refused to have her near me at all. Nothing could convince me that it was Grandmother. This was put down to delirium, but I do not think it was. I was quite conscious at the time. It was rather the fixed impression made on my mind in its weak state by what Father had told me. Grandmother *had* gone home, I reasoned, hence, she could *not* be there. *Therefore*, the woman who looked like her must be some one else.

It was not until I was able to sit up that I got over this delusion. One evening it simply dawned on me that it really was Grandmother. I was so happy, and could not bear to be out of her arms. I kept stroking her face constantly and saying in amazement and delight, "Why, you're *not* Mrs. Murphy, after all; you *are* Grandma."

Typhoid fever patients were not dieted so strictly during convalescence in those days as they are now. I remember one day, long before I was able to sit up, and only a short time after the fever had left me, that my dinner consisted of fried sausages—rich, pungent, savoury, home made sausages, such as are never found in these degenerate days. It was the first day that I had felt hungry, and I ate ravenously. Of course, by all the rules of the game, those sausages should have killed me, and so cut short that "career" of which I am writing. But they did not. These things are fated. I am sure that nothing short of pre-destination saved me from the consequences of those sausages.

Two incidents of the following summer stand out in my memory, probably because they were so keenly and so understandably bitter. One day I heard Grandmother reading from a newspaper an item to the effect that the end of the world was to come the following Sunday. At that time I had a most absolute and piteous belief in everything that was "printed." Whatever was in a newspaper must be true. I have lost this touching faith, I regret to say, and life is the poorer by the absence of many thrills of delight and horror.

From the time I heard that awesome prediction until Sunday was over I lived in an agony of terror and dread. The grown-up folk laughed at me, and refused to take my questions seriously. Now, I was almost as much afraid of being laughed at as of the Judgment Day. But all through the Saturday before that fateful Sunday I vexed Aunt Emily to distraction by repeatedly asking her if we should go to Sunday-school the next afternoon. Her assurance that of course we should go was a considerable comfort to me. If she really expected that there would be Sunday-school she could not believe that the next day would see the end of the world.

But then—it had been *printed*. That night was a time of intense wretchedness for me. Sleep was entirely out of the question. Might I not hear "the last trump" at any moment? I can laugh at it now—anyone would laugh. But it was real torture to a credulous child, just as real as any mental agony in after life.

Sunday was even more interminable than Sundays usually were, then. But it came to an end at last, and as its "dark, descending sun" dimpled the purple sky-line of the Gulf, I drew a long breath of relief. The beautiful green world of blossom and sunshine had not been burned up; it was going to last for a while longer. But I never forgot the suffering of that Sunday.

Many years later I used the incident as the foundation of the chapter "The Judgment Sunday" in *The Story Girl*. But the children of King Orchard had the sustaining companionship of each other. I had trodden the wine-press alone.

The other incident was much more trifling. The "Martin Forbes" of *The Story Girl* had his prototype in an old man who visited at my grandfather's for a week. Forbes was not his name, of course. He was, I believe, an amiable, respectable, and respected, old gentleman. But he won my undying hatred by calling me "Johnny" every time he spoke to me.

How I raged at him! It seemed to me a most deadly and unforgivable insult. My anger amused him hugely and incited him to persist in using the objectionable name. I could have torn that man in pieces had I had the power! When he went away I refused to shake hands with him, whereupon he laughed uproariously and said, "Oh, well, I won't call you 'Johnny' any more. After this I'll call you 'Sammy,' " which was, of course, adding fuel to the fire.

For years I couldn't hear that man's name without a sense of hot anger. Fully five years afterward, when I was ten, I remember writing this in my diary: "Mr. James Forbes is dead. He is the brother of a horrid man in Summerside who called me 'Johnny.'"

I never saw poor old Mr. Forbes again, so I never had to endure the indignity of being called "Sammy." He is now dead himself, and I daresay the fact that he called me "Johnny" was not brought up in judgment against him. Yet he may have committed what might be considered far greater sins that yet would not inflict on anyone a tithe of the humiliation which his teasing inflicted on a child's sensitive mind.

That experience taught me one lesson, at least. I never tease a child. If I had any tendency to do so, I should certainly be prevented by the still keen recollection of what I suffered at Mr. Forbes' hands. To him, it was merely the "fun" of teasing a "touchy" child. To me, it was the poison of asps.

❧ Chapter Three ❧

THE NEXT SUMMER, when I was six, I began to go to school. The Cavendish schoolhouse was a white-washed, low-eaved building on the side of the road just outside our gate. To the west and south was a spruce grove, covering a sloping hill. That old spruce grove, with its sprinkling of maple, was a fairy realm of beauty and romance to my childish imagination, I shall always be thankful that my school was near a grove—a place with winding paths and treasure-trove of ferns and mosses and wood-flowers. It was a stronger and better educative influence in my life than the lessons learned at the desk in the school-house.

And there was a brook in it, too—a delightful brook, with a big, deep, clear spring—where we went for buckets of water, and no end of pools and nooks where the pupils put their bottles of milk to keep sweet and cold until dinner hour. Each pupil had his or her own particular place, and woe betide a lad or lass who usurped another's prescriptive spot. I, alas, had no rights in the brook. Not for me was the pleasure of "scooting" down the winding path before school-time to put my bottle against a mossy log, where the sunlit water might dance and ripple against its creamy whiteness.

I had to go home to my dinner every day, and I was scandalously ungrateful for the privilege. Of course, I realize now that I was very fortunate in being able to go home every day for a good, warm dinner. But I could not see it in that light then. It was not half so interesting as taking lunch to school and eating it in sociable rings on the playground, or in groups under the trees. Great was my delight on those few stormy winter days when I had to take my dinner, too. I was "one of the crowd" then, not set apart in any lonely distinction of superior advantages.

Another thing that worried me with a sense of unlikeness was the fact that I was never allowed to go to school barefooted. All the other children went so, and I felt that this was a humiliating difference. At home I could run barefoot, but in school I must wear "buttoned boots." Not long ago, a girl who went to school with me confessed that she had always envied me those "lovely buttoned boots." Human nature always desirous of what it has not got! There was I, aching to go barefoot like my mates; there were they, resentfully thinking it was bliss to wear buttoned boots!

I do not think that the majority of grown-ups have any real conception of the tortures sensitive children suffer over any marked difference between themselves and the other denizens of their small world. I remember one winter I was sent to school wearing a new style of apron. I think still that it was rather ugly. *Then* I thought it was hideous. It was a long, sack-like garment, with *sleeves*. Those sleeves were the crowning indignity. Nobody in school had ever worn aprons with sleeves before. When I went to school one of the girls sneeringly remarked that they were *baby aprons*. This capped all! I could not bear to wear them, but wear them I had to. The humiliation never grew less. To the end of their existence, and they *did* wear horribly well, those "baby" aprons marked for me the extreme limit of human endurance.

I have no especial remembrance of my first day in school. Aunt Emily took me down to the school-house and gave me into the charge of some of the "big girls," with whom I sat that day. But my second day—ah! I shall not forget it while life lasts. I was late and had to go in alone. Very shyly I slipped in and sat down beside a "big girl." At once a wave of laughter rippled over the room. *I had come in with my hat on.*

As I write, the fearful shame and humiliation I endured at that moment rushes over me again. I felt that I was a target for the ridicule of the universe. Never, I felt certain, could I live down such a dreadful mistake. I crept out to take off my hat, a crushed morsel of humanity.

My novelty with the "big girls"—they were ten years old and seemed all but grown-up to me—soon grew stale, and I gravitated down to the girls of my own age. We "did" sums, and learned the multiplication table, and wrote "copies," and read lessons, and repeated spellings. I could read and write when I went to school. There must have been a time when I learned, as a first step into an enchanted world, that A was A; but for all the recollection I have of the process I might as well have been born with a capacity for reading, as we are for breathing and eating.

I was in the second book of the old Royal Reader series. I had gone through the primer at home with all its cat and rat formulae, and then had gone into the Second Reader, thus skipping the First Reader. When I went to school and found that there was a First Reader I felt greatly aggrieved to think that I had never gone through it. I seemed to have missed something, to suffer, in my own estimation, at least, a certain loss of standing because I had never had it. To this day there is a queer, absurd regret in my soul over missing that First Reader.

Life, from my seventh year, becomes more distinct in remembrance. In the winter following my seventh birthday, Aunt Emily married and went away, I remember her wedding as a most exciting event, as well as the weeks of mysterious preparation before; all the baking and frosting and decorating of cakes which went on! Aunt Emily was only a young girl then, but in my eyes she was as ancient as all the other grown-ups. I had no conception of age at that time. Either you were grown-up or you were not, that was all there was about it.

The wedding was one of the good, old-fashioned kind that is not known nowadays. All the big "connection" on both sides were present, the ceremony at seven o'clock, supper immediately afterward, then dancing and games, with another big supper at one o'clock.

For once I was permitted to stay up, probably because there was no place where I could be put to bed, every room being used for some gala purpose, and between excitement and unwatched indulgence in good things I was done up for a week. But it was worth it! Also, I regret to say, I pounded my new uncle with my fists and told him I hated him because he was taking Aunt Emily away.

The next summer two little boys came to board at my grandfather's and attend school, Wellington and David Nelson, better known as "Well" and "Dave." Well was just my age, Dave a year younger. They were my playmates for three happy years; we *did* have fun in abundance, simple, wholesome, delightful fun, with our playhouses and our games in the beautiful summer twilights, when we ranged happily through fields and orchards, or in the long winter evenings by the fire.

The first summer they came we built a playhouse in the spruce grove to the west of our front orchard. It was in a little circle of young spruces. We built our house by driving stakes into the ground between the trees, and lacing fir boughs in and out. I was especially expert at this, and always won the boys' admiration by my knack of filling up obstreperous holes in our verdant castle. We also manufactured a door for it, a very rickety affair, consisting of three rough boards nailed uncertainly across two others, and hung to a long-suffering birch tree by ragged leather hinges cut from old boots. But that door was as beautiful and precious in our eyes as the Gate Beautiful of the Temple was to the Jews of old. You see, we had made it ourselves!

Then we had a little garden, our pride and delight, albeit it rewarded all our labour very meagrely. We planted live-forevers around all our beds, and they grew as only live-forevers *can* grow. They were almost the only things that *did* grow. Our carrots and parsnips, our lettuces and beets, our phlox and sweetpeas—either failed to come up at all, or dragged a pallid, spindling existence to an ignoble end, in spite of all our patient digging, manuring, weeding, and watering, or, perhaps, because of it, for I fear we were more zealous than wise. But we worked persistently, and took our consolation out of a few hardy sunflowers which, sown in an uncared-for spot, throve better than all our petted darlings, and lighted up a corner of the spruce grove with their cheery golden lamps. I remember we were in great tribulation because our beans persisted in coming up with their skins over their heads. We promptly picked them off, generally with disastrous consequences to the beans.

Readers of *Anne of Green Gables* will remember the Haunted Wood. It was a gruesome fact to us three young imps. Well and Dave had a firm and rooted belief in ghosts. I used to argue with them over it with the depressing result that I became infected myself. Not that I really believed in ghosts, pure and simple; but I was inclined to agree with Hamlet that there might be more things in heaven and earth than were commonly dreamed of—in the philosophy of Cavendish authorities, anyhow.

The Haunted Wood was a harmless, pretty spruce grove in the field below the orchard. We considered that all our haunts were too commonplace, so we invented this for our own amusement. None of us really believed at first, that the grove *was* haunted, or that the mysterious "white things" which we pretended to see flitting through it at dismal hours were aught but the creations of our own fancy. But our minds were weak and our imaginations strong; we soon came to believe implicitly in our myths, and not one of us would have gone near that grove after sunset on pain of death. Death! What was death compared to the unearthly possibility of falling into the clutches of a "white thing"?

In the evenings, when, as usual, we were perched on the back porch steps in the mellow summer dusk, Well would tell me blood-curdling tales galore, until my hair fairly stood on end, and I would not have been surprised had a whole army of "white things" swooped suddenly on us from round the corner. One tale was that his grandmother having gone out one evening to milk the cows, saw his grandfather, as she supposed, come out of the house, drive the cows into the yard and then go down the lane.

The "creep" of this story consisted in the fact that she went straightway into the house and found him lying on the sofa where she had left him, he having never been out of the house at all. Next day something happened to the poor old gentleman. I forget what, but doubtless it was some suitable punishment for sending his wraith out to drive cows!

Another story was that a certain dissipated youth of the community, going home one Saturday night, or rather Sunday morning, from some unhallowed orgy, was pursued by a lamb of fire, with its head cut off and hanging by a strip of skin or flame. For weeks afterward I could not go anywhere after dark without walking with my head over my shoulder, watching apprehensively for that fiery apparition.

One evening Dave came down to me in the apple orchard at dusk, with his eyes nearly starting out of his head, and whispered that he had heard a bell ringing in the then deserted house. To be sure, the marvellous edge was soon taken off this by the discovery that the noise was simply a newly-cleaned clock striking the hours, which it had never done before. This furnished the foundation of the "Ghostly Bell" chapter in *The Story Girl*.

But, one night we had a real ghost scare—the "real" qualifying "scare," not "ghost." We were playing at twilight in the hayfield south of the house, chasing each other around the fragrant coils of new-cut hay. Suddenly I happened to glance up in the direction of the orchard dyke. A chill began galloping up and down my spine, for there, under the juniper tree, was really a "white thing," shapelessly white in the gathering gloom. We all stopped and stared as though turned to stone.

"It's Mag Laird," whispered Dave in terrified tones.

Mag Laird, I may remark, was a harmless creature who wandered begging over the country side, and was the bug-bear of children in general and Dave in particular. As poor Mag's usual apparel was dirty, cast-off clothes of other persons, it did not seem to me likely that this white visitant were she. Well and I would have been glad to think it was, for Mag was at least flesh and blood while this—!

"Nonsense!" I said, trying desperately to be practical. "It must be the white calf."

Well agreed with me with suspicious alacrity, but the shapeless, grovelling thing did not look in the least like a calf.

"It's coming here!" he suddenly exclaimed in terror.

I gave one agonized glance. Yes! It was creeping down over the dyke, as no calf ever did or could creep. With a simultaneous shriek we started for the house, Dave gasping at every step, "It's Mag Laird," while all that Well and I could realize was that it was a "white thing" after us at last!

We reached the house and tore into Grandmother's bedroom, where we had left her sewing. She was not there. We swung round and stampeded for a neighbour's, where we arrived trembling in every limb. We gasped out our awful tale and were laughed at, of course. But no persuasion could induce us to go back, so the French-Canadian servants, Peter and Charlotte, set off to explore, one carrying a pail of oats, the other armed with a pitchfork.

They came back and announced that there was nothing to be seen. This did not surprise us. Of course, a "white thing" would vanish, when it had fulfilled its mission of scaring three wicked children out of their senses. But go home we would not until Grandfather appeared and marched us back in disgrace. For what do you think it was?

A white tablecloth had been bleaching on the grass under the juniper tree, and, just at dusk, Grandmother, knitting in hand, went out to get it. She flung the cloth over her shoulder and then her ball fell and rolled over the dyke. She knelt down and was reaching over to pick it up when she was arrested by our sudden stampede and shrieks of terror. Before she could move or call out we had disappeared.

So collapsed our last" ghost," and spectral terrors languished after that, for we were laughed at for many a long day.

But we played house and gardened and swung and picnicked and climbed trees. How we did love trees! I am grateful that my childhood was spent in a spot where there were many trees, trees of personality, planted and tended by hands long dead, bound up with everything of joy or sorrow that visited our lives. When I have "lived with" a tree for many years it seems to me like a beloved human companion.

Behind the barn grew a pair of trees I always called "The Lovers," a spruce and a maple, and so closely intertwined that the boughs of the spruce were literally woven into the boughs of the maple. I remember that I wrote a poem about them and called it "The Tree Lovers." They lived in happy union for many years. The maple died first; the spruce held her dead form in his green, faithful arms for two more years. But his heart was broken and he died too. They were beautiful in their lives and in death not long divided; and they nourished a child's heart with a grace-giving fancy.

In a corner of the front orchard grew a beautiful young birch tree. I named it "The White Lady," and had a fancy about it to the effect that it was the beloved of all the dark spruces near, and that they were rivals for her love. It was the whitest straightest thing ever seen, young and fair and maiden-like.

On the southern edge of the Haunted Wood grew a most magnificent old birch. This was the tree of trees to me. I worshipped it, and called it "The Monarch of The Forest." One of my earliest "poems"—the third I wrote—was written on it, when I was nine. Here is all I remember of it:

"Around the poplar and the spruce
  The fir and maple stood;
But the old tree that I loved the best
  Grew in the Haunted Wood,

It was a stately, tall old birch,
  With spreading branches green;
It kept off heat and sun and glare—
  'Twas a goodly tree, I ween.

'Twas the Monarch of the Forest,
  A splendid kingly name,
Oh, it was a beautiful birch tree,
  A tree that was known to fame."

The last line was certainly a poetic fiction, Oliver Wendell Holmes says:

"There's nothing that keeps its youth,
So far as I know, but a tree and truth."

But even a tree does not live forever, The Haunted Wood was cut down. The big birch was left standing, But, deprived of the shelter of the thick-growing spruces, it gradually died before the bitter northern blasts from the Gulf. Every spring more of its boughs failed to leaf out. The poor tree stood like a discrowned, forsaken king in a ragged cloak, I was not sorry when it was finally cut down. "The land of dreams among," it resumed its sceptre and reigns in fadeless beauty.

Every apple tree in the two orchards had its own individuality and name—"Aunt Emily's tree," "Uncle Leander's tree," the "Little Syrup tree," the "Spotty tree," the "Spider tree," the "Gavin tree," and many others. The "Gavin" tree bore small, whitish-green apples, and was so called because a certain small boy named Gavin, hired on a neighbouring farm, had once been caught stealing them. Why the said Gavin should have imperiled his soul and lost his reputation by electing to steal apples from that especial tree I could never understand, for they were hard, bitter, flavourless things, good neither for eating or cooking.

Dear old trees! I hope they all had souls and will grow again for me on the hills of Heaven. I want, in some future life, to meet the old "Monarch" and the "White Lady," and even poor, dishonest little "Gavin's tree" again.

❧ Chapter Four ❧

WHEN I WAS eight years old Cavendish had a very exciting summer, perhaps the most exciting summer it ever had, and of course we children revelled in the excitement. The *Marcopolo* was wrecked on the sandshore.

The *Marcopolo* was a very famous old ship and the fastest sailing vessel of her class ever built. She had a strange, romantic history, and was the nucleus of many traditions and sailors' yarns. She had finally been condemned in England under the Plimsoll Bill. Her owners evaded the Bill by selling her to a Norwegian firm, and then chartering her to bring a cargo of deal plank from Quebec. On her return she was caught in a furious storm out in the Gulf, sprung a leak, and became so water-logged that the captain determined to run her on shore to save crew and cargo.

That day we had a terrible windstorm in Cavendish. Suddenly the news was spread that a vessel was coming ashore. Everyone who could rushed to the sandshore and saw a magnificent sight!—a large vessel coming straight on before the northern gale with every stitch of canvas set. She grounded about three hundred yards from the shore and as she struck the crew cut the rigging, and the huge masts went over with a crash that was heard for a mile, above the roaring of the storm.

The next day the crew of twenty men got ashore and found boarding places about Cavendish. Being typical tars, they painted our quiet settlement a glowing scarlet for the remainder of the summer. It was their especial delight to crowd into a truck-wagon, and go galloping along the roads yelling at the top of their voices. They were of many nationalities, Irishmen, Englishmen, Scotchmen, Spaniards, Norwegians, Swedes, Dutchmen, Germans, and—most curious of all—two Tahitians, whose woolly heads, thick lips, and gold earrings were a never-failing joy to Well and Dave and me.

There was an immense amount of red tape in connection with the affair, and the *Marcopolo* men were in Cavendish for weeks. The captain boarded with us. He was a Norwegian, a delightful, gentlemanly old fellow who was idolized by his crew. He spoke English well, but was apt to get rather mixed up in his prepositions.

"Thank you for your kindness *against* me, little Miss Maud," he would say with a grand bow.

Owing to the presence of the captain, the crew haunted our domain also. I remember the night they were all paid off: they all sat out on the grass under the parlour windows, feeding our old dog Gyp with biscuits. Well and Dave and I saw, with eyes as big as owls', the parlour table literally covered with gold sovereigns, which the captain paid out to the men. Never had we imagined there was so much wealth in the world.

Naturally the shore was a part of my life from my earliest consciousness. I learned to know it and love it in every mood. The Cavendish shore is a very beautiful one; part of it is rock shore, where the rugged red cliffs rise steeply from the boulder-strewn coves. Part is a long, gleaming sandshore, divided from the fields and ponds behind by a row of rounded sand-dunes, covered by coarse sand-hill grass. This sandshore is a peerless spot for bathing.

All through my childhood I spent much of my time on the shore. It was not so quiet and solitary then as it is today. Those were the days when the mackerel fishing was good, and the shore was dotted with fishing houses. Many of the farmers had a fishing house on the shore field of their farms, with a boat drawn up on the skids below. Grandfather always fished mackerel in the summer, his boat manned by two or three French Canadians, fishing on the shores. Just where the rocks left off and the sandshore began was quite a little colony of fishing houses. The place was called Cawnpore, owing to the fact that on the day and hour when the last nail was being driven into the last house news arrived of the massacre of Cawnpore in the Indian Mutiny. There is not a house left there now.

The men would get up at three or four in the morning and go out fishing. Then we children had to take their breakfast down at eight, later on their dinner, and, if the fish "schooled" all day, their supper also. In vacations we would spend most of the day there, and I soon came to know every cove, headland, and rock on that shore. We would watch the boats through the sky-glass, paddle in the water, gather shells and pebbles and mussels, and sit on the rocks and eat dulse, literally, by the yard. The rocks at low tide were covered by millions of snails, as we called them. I think the correct name is periwinkle. We often found great, white, empty "snail" shells, as big as our fists, that had been washed ashore from some distant strand or deep sea haunt. I early learned by heart, Holmes' beautiful lines on "The Chambered Nautilus," and I rather fancied myself sitting dreamily on a big boulder with my bare, wet feet tucked up under my print skirt, holding a huge "snail" shell in my sunburned paw and appealing to my soul to "build thee more stately mansions."

There were many "outgrown shells" by that "unresting sea," and we carried them home to add to our collection, or to encircle our flower beds. Up by the sea run, where the ponds empty into the Gulf, we always found beautiful, white, quahog-clam shells galore.

The waves constantly dashing against the soft sandstone cliffs wore them away into many beautiful arches and caves. Somewhat to the east of our fishing house was a bold headland against which the water lapped at lowest tide. Through the neck of this headland a hole became worn—a hole so small that we could scarcely thrust a hand through it. Every season it grew a little larger. One summer an adventurous school chum and I crawled through it. It was a tight squeeze, and we used to exult with a fearful joy over having dared it, and speculate as to what would have happened if one of us had got stuck half-way through!

In a few more years we could walk upright through the opening. Then a horse and carriage could have been driven through it. Finally, in about fifteen years from the beginning the thin bridge of rock at the top gave way, and the headland became an island, as though a gateway had been cleft through its wall.

There were many stories and legends connected with the shore, of which I heard older persons talk. Grandfather liked a dramatic story, had a good memory for its fine points, and could tell it well. He had many tales to relate of the terrible American gale—or "Yankee storm," as it was called—when hundreds of American fishing vessels out in the Gulf were wrecked upon the north shore.

The story of the *Franklin Dexter* and the four brothers who sailed in her, which is related in *The Golden Road*, is literally true. Grandfather was among those who found the bodies, helped to bury them in Cavendish churchyard, helped to take them up when the broken-hearted old father came, and helped to put them on the ill-fated *Seth Hall*.

Then there was the story of Cape Leforce, a bit of tragic, unwritten history harking back to the days when the "Island of St. John" belonged to France. It was some time in the 1760s. I can never remember dates. The only two dates which remain in my memory out of all those so painstakingly learned in schooldays are that Julius Caesar landed in England 55 B.C. and the Battle of Waterloo was fought in 1815. France and England were at war. French privateers infested the Gulf sallying therefrom to plunder the commerce of the New England Colonies. One of these was commanded by a captain named Leforce.

One night they anchored off the Cavendish shore, at that time an unnamed, wooded solitude. For some reason the crew came ashore and camped for the night on the headland now known as Cape Leforce. The captain and his mate shared a tent, and endeavoured to come to a division of their booty. They quarrelled, and it was arranged that they should fight a duel at sunrise. But in the morning, as the ground was being paced off, the mate suddenly raised his pistol and shot Captain Leforce dead.

I do not know if the mate was ever punished for this deed. Probably not. It was a mere brief sentence in a long page of bloodshed. But the captain was buried by his crew on the spot where he fell, and I have often heard Grandfather say that *his* father had seen the grave in his boyhood. It had long ago crumbled off into the waves, but the name still clings to the red headland.

A way to the westward, six or seven miles the view was bounded by New London Cape, a long, sharp point, running far out to sea. In my childhood I never wearied of speculating what was on the other side of that point, a very realm of enchantment, surely, I thought. Even when I gradually drew into the understanding that beyond it was merely another reach of shore like my own it still held a mystery and a fascination for me. I longed to stand out on that lonely, remote, purple point, beyond which was the land of lost sunsets.

I have seen few more beautiful sights than sea-sunset off that point. In later years a new charm was added, a revolving light that flashed like a magnificent star through the dusk of summer nights, like a beacon on an outpost of fairyland.

I did not often fare far afield. An occasional trip to town—Charlottetown—and another to Uncle John Campbell's at Park Corner, were my only excursions beyond my horizon line, and both were looked on as great pleasures. A trip to Park Corner was of comparatively frequent occurrence, once a year at least, and perhaps twice. A trip to town was a very rare treat, once in three years, and loomed up in about the same proportions of novelty, excitement, and delight as a trip to Europe would now—or before the war. It meant a brief sojourn in a wonderful and fascinating place, where everyone was dressed up and could have all the nuts, candies, and oranges they wanted, to say nothing of the exquisite pleasure of looking at all the beautiful things in the shop windows.

I remember distinctly my first trip to town at the age of five. I had a glorious day, but the most delightful part was a tiny adventure I had just before leaving for home. Grandfather and Grandmother had met some friends at a street corner and stopped to talk. Finding that I wasn't being looked after, I promptly shot down a near-by side street, agog for adventures. It was *so* jolly and independent to be walking down a street all alone. It was a wonderful street, I've never seen it since—not with the same eyes, anyway. No other street has ever had the charm that one had. The most amazing sight I saw was a woman shaking rugs on *the top of a house*. I felt dizzy with astonishment over such a topsy-turvy sight. *We* shook rugs in the yard. Who ever heard of shaking them on the top of a house!

Arriving at the bottom of the street I coolly ran down the steps of an open door I found there, and discovered myself to be in a charming dim spot, full of barrels, with a floor ankle-deep with beautiful curly shavings. But, seeing someone moving in a distant corner I was overcome, not by fear but by shyness, and beat a hasty retreat. On my way back I met a little girl with a pitcher in her hand. We both stopped, and with the instinctive, unconventional *camaraderie* of childhood plunged into an intimate, confidential conversation. She was a jolly little soul, with black eyes and two long braids of black hair. We told each other how old we were, and how many dolls we had, and almost everything else there was to tell except our names which neither of us thought about. When we parted, I felt as though I were leaving a life long friend. We never met again.

When I rejoined my grown-ups they had not missed me at all, and knew nothing of my rapturous voyage into Wonderland.

The Park Corner jaunts were always delightful. To begin with, it was such a pretty drive, those winding thirteen miles through hill and wood, and by river and shore. There were many bridges to cross, two of them, with drawbridges. I was always horribly frightened of drawbridges, and am to this day.

Do what I will, I cringe secretly from the time the horse steps on the bridge until I am safely over the draw.

Uncle John Campbell's house was a big white one, smothered in orchards. Here, in other days, there was a trio of merry cousins to rush out and drag me in with greeting and laughter. The very walls of that house must have been permeated by the essence of good times. And there was a famous old pantry, always stored with goodies, into which it was our habit to crowd at bedtime and devour unholy snacks with sounds of riot and mirth.

There is a certain old screw sticking out from the wall on the stair landing which always makes me realize clearly that I am really grown-up. When I used to visit at Park Corner in the dawn of memory that screw was just on a level with my nose! *Now*, it comes to my knees. I used to measure myself by it every time I went over.

I was very fond of trouting and berry picking. We fished the brooks up in the woods, using the immemorial hook and line, with "w'ums" for bait. Generally I managed to put my worm on myself, but I expended a fearful amount of nervous energy in doing it. However, I managed to catch fish. I remember the thrill of pride I felt one day when I caught quite a large trout, as large as some of the grown-ups had caught in the pond. Well and Dave were with me, and I felt that I went up five per cent, in their estimation. A girl who could catch a trout like that was not to be altogether despised.

We picked berries in the wild lands and fields back of the woods, going to them through wooded lanes fragrant with June bells, threaded with sunshine and shadow, carpeted with mosses, where we saw foxes and rabbits in their native haunts. I have never heard anything sweeter than the whistling of the robins at sunset in the maple woods around those fields.

To go through woods with company was very pleasant; to go through them alone was a very different thing. A mile in along the road lived a family who kept a small shop where they sold tea and sugar, etc. I was frequently sent in to buy some household supplies, and I shall never forget the agony of terror I used to endure going through those woods. The distance through the woods was not more than a quarter of a mile, but it seemed endless to me.

I cannot tell just what I was afraid of. I *knew* there was nothing in the wood worse than rabbits or as the all-wise grown-ups told me "worse than yourself." It was just the old, primitive fear handed down to me from ancestors who, in the dawn of time, were afraid of the woods with good reason. With me, it was a blind, unreasoning terror. And this was in daylight; to go through those woods *after dark* was something simply unthinkable. There were persons who did it. A young schoolmaster who boarded with us thought nothing apparently of walking through them at night. In my eyes he was the greatest hero the world had ever seen!

❦ Chapter Five ❦

I HAVE SPOKEN of the time I realized physical pain. My first realization of the mental pain of sorrow came when I was nine years old.

I had two pet kittens, Catkin and Pussy-willow. Catkin was a little too meek and pink-nosed to suit me, but Pussy-willow was the prettiest, "cutest" little scrap of gray-striped fur ever seen and I loved her passionately.

One morning I found her dying of poison. I shall never forget my agony of grief as I watched my little pet's bright eyes glazing, and her tiny paws growing stiff and cold. And I have never laughed with grown-up wisdom at my passionate sorrow over the little death. It was too real, too symbolical! It was the first time I *realized* death, the first time, since I had become conscious of loving, that anything I loved had left me forever. At that moment the curse of the race came upon me, "death entered into my world" and I turned my back on the Eden of childhood where everything had seemed everlasting. I was barred out of it forevermore by the fiery sword of that keen and unforgettable pain.

We were Presbyterians, and went every Sunday to the old Cavendish Presbyterian Church on the bleak hill. It was never a handsome church, inside or out, but it was beautified in its worshippers' eyes by years of memories and sacred associations. Our pew was by a window and we looked out over the slope of the long western hill and the blue pond down to the curving rim of the sand hills and the fine sweep of the blue Gulf.

There was a big gallery at the back of the church. I always hankered to sit there, principally because I wasn't allowed to, no doubt, another instance of forbidden fruit! Once a year, on Sacrament Sunday, I was permitted to go up there with the other girls, and I considered it a great treat. We could look down over the whole congregation, which always flowered out that day in full bloom of new hats and dresses. Sacrament Sunday, then, was to us what Easter is to the dwellers in cities. We all had new hats or dresses, sometimes, oh, bliss, we had both! And I very much fear that we thought more about them than we did about the service and what it commemorated. It was rather a long service in those days, and we small fry used to get very tired and rather inclined to envy certain irresponsible folk who went out while the congregation sang " 'Twas on that night when doomed to know." We liked the Sunday School much better than the church services. Some of my sweetest memories are of the hours spent in that old church with my little mates, with our testaments and lesson sheets held in our cotton-gloved hands. Saturday night we had been made to learn our catechism and our Golden texts and our paraphrases. I always enjoyed reciting those paraphrases, particularly any that had dramatic lines.

The London *Spectator*, in a very kind review of *Anne of Green Gables* said that possibly Anne's precocity was slightly overdrawn in the statement that a child of eleven could appreciate the dramatic effect of the lines,

"Quick as the slaughtered squadrons fell
    In Midian's evil day."

But I was only nine when those lines thrilled my very soul as I recited them in Sunday School. All through the sermon following I kept repeating them to myself. To this day they give me a mysterious pleasure and a pleasure quite independent of their meaning.

So ran the current of my life in childhood, very quiet and simple, you perceive. Nothing at all exciting about it, nothing that savours of a "career." Some might think it dull. But life never held for me a dull moment. I had, in my vivid imagination, a passport to the geography of Fairyland. In a twinkling I could—and did—whisk myself into regions of wonderful adventures, unhampered by any restrictions of time or place.

Everything was invested with a kind of fairy grace and charm, emanating from my own fancy, the trees that whispered nightly around the old house where I slept, the woodsy nooks I explored, the homestead fields, each individualized by some oddity of fence or shape, the sea whose murmur was never out of my ears—all were radiant with "the glory and the dream."

I had always a deep love of nature. A little fern growing in the woods, a shallow sheet of June-bells under the firs, moonlight falling on the ivory column of a tall birch, an evening star over the old tamarack on the dyke, shadow-waves rolling over a field of ripe wheat—all gave me "thoughts that lay too deep for tears" and feelings which I had then no vocabulary to express.

It has always seemed to me, ever since early childhood, that, amid all the commonplaces of life, I was very near to a kingdom of ideal beauty. Between it and me hung only a thin veil. I could never draw it quite aside, but sometimes a wind fluttered it and I caught a glimpse of the enchanting realm beyond—only a glimpse—but those glimpses have always made life worth while.

It goes without saying that I was passionately fond of reading. We did not have a great many books in the house, but there were generally plenty of papers and a magazine or two. Grandmother took *Godey's Lady's Book*. I do not know if I would think much of that magazine now, but then I thought it wonderful, and its monthly advents were epochs to me. The opening pages were full of fashion plates and were a perpetual joy; I hung over them with delight, and whiled away many an hour choosing what frocks I would have if I could. Those were the days of bangs, bristles, and high-crowned hats, all of which I considered extremely beautiful and meant to have as soon as I was old enough. Beyond the fashion pages came the literary pabulum, short stories and serials, which I devoured ravenously, crying my eyes out in delicious woe over the agonies of the heroines who were all superlatively beautiful and good. Everyone in fiction was either black or white in those days. There were no grays. The villains and villainesses were all neatly labelled and you were sure of your ground. The old method had its merits. Nowadays it is quite hard to tell which is the villain and which the hero. But there was never any doubt in *Godey's Lady's Book*. What books we had were well and often read. I had my especial favourites. There were two red-covered volumes of *A History of the World*, with crudely-coloured pictures, which were a never-failing delight. I fear that, as history, they were rather poor stuff, but as story books they were very interesting. They began with Adam and Eve in Eden, went through "the glory that was Greece and the grandeur that was Rome," down to Victoria's reign.

Then there was a missionary book dealing with the Pacific Islands, in which I revelled because it was full of pictures of cannibal chiefs with the most extraordinary hair arrangements. Hans Andersen's Tales were a perennial joy. I always loved fairy tales and delighted in ghost stories. Indeed, to this day I like nothing better than a well-told ghost story, warranted to send a cold creep down your spine. But it must be a real ghost story, mark you. The spook must not turn out a delusion and a snare.

I did not have access to many novels. Those were the days when novels were frowned on as reading for children. The only novels in the house were *Rob Roy*, *Pickwick Papers*, and Bulwer Lytton's *Zanoni*; and I pored over them until I knew whole chapters by heart.

Fortunately poetry did not share the ban of novels. I could revel at will in Longfellow, Tennyson, Whittier, Scott, Byron, Milton, Burns. Poetry pored over in childhood becomes part of one's nature more thoroughly than that which if first read in mature years can ever do. Its music was woven into my growing soul and has echoed through it, consciously and subconsciously, ever since: "the music of the immortals, of those great, beautiful souls whose passing tread has made of earth holy ground."

But even poetry was barred on Sundays. Then our faithful standbys were *Pilgrim's Progress* and Talmage's *Sermons*. *Pilgrim's Progress* was read and re-read with never-failing delight. I am proud of this; but I am not quite so proud of the fact that I found just as much delight in reading Talmage's *Sermons*. That was Talmage's palmy day. All the travelling colporteurs carried his books, and a new volume of Talmage's meant then to us pretty much what a "bestseller" does now. I cannot claim that it was the religion that attracted me, though at that age I liked the Talmage brand much; it was the anecdotes and the vivid, dramatic word-pictures. His sermons were as interesting as fiction. I am sure I couldn't read them with any patience now; but I owe Talmage a very real debt of thanks for pleasure given to a child craving the vividness of life.

My favourite Sunday book, however, was a thin little volume entitled *The Memoir of Anzonetta Peters*. I shall never forget that book. It belonged to a type now vanished from the earth—fortunately—but much in vogue at that time. It was the biography of a child who at five years became converted, grew very ill soon afterward, lived a marvellously patient and saintly life for several years, and died, after great sufferings, at the age of ten.

I must have read that book a hundred times if I did once. I don't think it had a good effect on me. For one thing it discouraged me horribly. Anzonetta was so hopelessly perfect that I felt it was no use to try to imitate her. Yet I did try. She never seemed by any chance to use the ordinary language of childhood at all. She invariably responded to any remark, if it were only "How are you today, Anzonetta?" by quoting a verse of scripture or a hymn stanza. Anzonetta was a perfect hymnal. She died to a hymn, her last, faintly-whispered utterance being

"Hark, they whisper, angels say,
Sister spirit, come away."

I dared not attempt to use verses and hymns in current conversation. I had a wholesome conviction that I should be laughed at, and moreover, I doubted being understood. But I did my best; I wrote hymn after hymn in my little diary, and patterned the style of my entries after Anzonetta's remarks.

For example, I remember writing gravely "I wish I were in Heaven now, with Mother and George Whitefield and Anzonetta B. Peters."

But I didn't really wish it. I only thought I *ought* to. I was, in reality, very well contented with my own world, and my own little life full of cabbages and kings.

❦ Chapter Six ❧

I HAVE WRITTEN at length about the incidents and environment of my childhood because they had a marked influence on the development of my literary gift. A different environment would have given it a different bias. Were it not for those Cavendish years, I do not think *Anne of Green Gables* would ever have been written.

When I am asked "When did you begin to write?" I say, "I wish I could remember." I cannot remember the time when I was not writing, or when I did not mean to be an author. To write has always been my central purpose around which every effort and hope and ambition of my life has grouped itself. I was an indefatigable little scribbler, and stacks of manuscripts, long ago reduced to ashes, alas, bore testimony to the same. I wrote about all the little incidents of my existence. I wrote descriptions of my favourite haunts, biographies of my many cats, histories of visits, and school affairs, and even critical reviews of the books I had read.

One wonderful day, when I was nine years old, I discovered that I could write poetry. I had been reading Thomson's Seasons, of which a little black, curly-covered atrociously printed copy had fallen into my hands. So I composed a "poem" called "Autumn" in blank verse in imitation thereof. I wrote it, I remember, on the back of one of the long red "letter bills" then used in the postal service. It was seldom easy for me to get all the paper I wanted, and those blessed old letter bills were positive boons. Grandfather kept the post office, and three times a week a discarded "letter bill" came my grateful way. The Government was not so economical then as now, at least in the matter of letter bills; they were then half a yard long.

As for "Autumn," I remember only the opening lines:

"Now autumn comes, laden with peach and pear;
The sportsman's horn is heard throughout the land,
And the poor partridge, fluttering, falls dead."

True, peaches and pears were not abundant in Prince Edward Island at any season, and I am sure nobody ever heard a "sportsman's horn" in that Province, though there really was some partridge shooting. But in those glorious days my imagination refused to be hampered by facts. Thomson had sportsman's horns and so forth; therefore I must have them too.

Father came to see me the very day I wrote it, and I proudly read it to him. He remarked unenthusiastically that "it didn't sound much like poetry." This squelched me for a time; but if the love of writing is bred in your bones, you will be practically non-squelchable. Once I had found out that I could write poetry I overflowed into verse over everything. I wrote in rhyme after that, though, having concluded that it was because "Autumn" did not rhyme that Father thought it wasn't poetry. I wrote yards of verses about flowers and months and trees and stars and sunsets, and I addressed "Lives" to my friends.

A school chum of mine, Alma M—, had also a knack of writing rhyme. She and I had a habit, no doubt, a reprehensible one, of getting out together on the old side bench at school, and writing "po'try" on our slates, when the master fondly supposed we were sharpening our intellects on fractions.

We began by first writing acrostics on our names; then we wrote poems addressed to each other in which we praised each other fulsomely; finally, one day, we agreed to write up in stirring rhyme all our teachers, including the master himself. We filled our slates; two verses were devoted to each teacher, and the two concerning the reigning pedagogue were very sarcastic effusions dealing with some of his flirtations with the Cavendish belles. Alma and I were gleefully comparing our productions when the master himself, who had been standing before us but with his back toward us, hearing a class, suddenly wheeled about and took my slate out of my paralyzed hand. Horrors! I stood up, firmly believing that the end of all things was at hand. Why he did not read it I do not know, it may be he had a dim suspicion what it was and wanted to save his dignity. Whatever his reason, he handed the slate back to me in silence, and I sat down with a gasp, sweeping off the accusing words as I did so lest he might change his mind. Alma and I were so badly scared that we gave up at once and forever the stolen delight of writing poetry in company on the side bench!

I remember—who could ever forget it?—the first commendation my writing received. I was about twelve and I had a stack of poems written out and hidden jealously from all eyes, for I was very sensitive in regard to my scribblings and could not bear the thought of having them seen and laughed at. Nevertheless, I wanted to know what others would think of them, not from vanity, but from a strong desire to find out if an impartial judge would see any merit in them. So I employed a little ruse to find out. It all seems very funny to me now, and a little pitiful; but then it seemed to me that I was at the bar of judgment for all time. It would be too much to say that, had the verdict been unfavourable, I would have forever surrendered my dreams, but they would certainly have been frosted for a time.

A lady was visiting us who was something of a singer. One evening I timidly asked her if she had ever heard a song called "Evening Dreams."

She certainly had not, for the said "Evening Dreams" was a poem of my own composition, which I then considered my masterpiece. It is not now extant, and I can remember the first two verses only. I suppose that they were indelibly impressed on my memory by the fact that the visitor asked me if I knew any of the words of the" song." Whereupon I, in a trembling voice, recited the two opening verses:

"When the evening sun is setting
    Quietly in the west,
In a halo of rainbow glory,
    I sit me down to rest.

I forget the present and future,
    I live over the past once more,
As I see before me crowding
    The beautiful days of yore."

Strikingly original! Also, a child of twelve would have a long "past" to live over!

I finished up with a positive gasp, but the visitor was busy with her fancy work, and did not notice my pallor and general shakiness. For I *was* pale, it was a moment of awful import to me. She placidly said that she had never heard the song, but "the words were very pretty."

The fact that she was sincere must certainly detract from her reputation for literary discrimination. But to me it was the sweetest morsel of commendation that had ever fallen to my lot, or that ever has fallen since, for that matter. Nothing has ever surpassed that delicious moment. I ran out of the house—it wasn't big enough to contain my joy, I must have all outdoors for that—and danced down the lane under the birches in a frenzy of delight, hugging to my heart the remembrance of those words.

Perhaps it was this that encouraged me sometime during the following winter to write out my "Evening Dreams" very painstakingly—on both sides of the paper, alas!—and to send them to the editor of *The Household*, an American magazine we took. The idea of being paid for them never entered my head. Indeed, I am not at all sure that I knew at that time that people were ever paid for writing. At least, my early dreams of literary fame were untainted by any mercenary speculations.

Alack! the editor of *The Household* was less complimentary than our visitor. He sent the verses back, although I had *not* "enclosed a stamp" for the purpose, being in blissful ignorance of any such requirement.

My aspirations were nipped in the bud for a time. It was a year before I recovered from the blow. Then I essayed a more modest flight. I copied out my "Evening Dreams" again and sent them to the Charlottetown *Examiner*. I felt quite sure it would print them, for it often printed verses which I thought, and, for that matter, still think, were no better than mine.

For a week I dreamed delicious dreams of seeing my verses in the Poet's Corner; with my name appended thereto. When the *Examiner* came, I opened it with tremulous eagerness. There was not a sign of an evening dream about it!

I drained the cup of failure to the very dregs. It seems very amusing to me now, but it was horribly real and tragic to me then. I was crushed in the very dust of humiliation and I had no hope of rising again. I burned my "Evening Dreams," and, although I continued to write because I couldn't help it, I sent no more poems to the editors.

Poems, however, were not all I wrote. Very soon after I began to write verses I also began to write stories. The "Story Club" in *Anne of Green Gables* was suggested by a little incident of schooldays when Janie S—, Amanda M— and I all wrote a story with the same plot. I remember only that it was a very tragic plot, and the heroines were all drowned while bathing on Cavendish sandshore! Oh, it was very sad! It was the first, and probably the last, time that Janie and Amanda attempted fiction, but I had already quite a library of stories in which almost everyone died. A certain lugubrious yarn, "My Graves," was my masterpiece. It was a long tale of the peregrinations of a Methodist minister's wife, who buried a child in every circuit to which she went. The oldest was buried in Newfoundland, the last in Vancouver, and all Canada between was dotted with those graves. I wrote the story in the first person, described the children, pictured out their death beds, and detailed their tombstones and epitaphs.

Then there was "This History of Flossy Brighteyes," the biography of a doll. I couldn't kill a doll, but I dragged her through every other tribulation. However, I allowed her to have a happy old age with a good little girl who loved her for the dangers she had passed and overlooked her consequent lack of beauty.

Nowadays, my reviewers say that my forte is humour. Well, there was not much humour in those early tales, at least, it was not intended there should be. Perhaps I worked all the tragedy out of my system in them, and left an unimpeded current of humour. I think it was my love of the dramatic that urged me to so much infanticide. In real life I couldn't have hurt a fly, and the thought that superfluous kittens had to be drowned was torture to me. But in my stories battle, murder and sudden death were the order of the day.

When I was fifteen I had my first ride on a railway train, and it was a long one. I went with Grandfather Montgomery to Prince Albert, Saskatchewan, where Father had married again and was then living. I spent a year in Prince Albert and attended the High School there.

It was now three years since I had suffered so much mortification over "Evening Dreams." By this time my long-paralyzed ambition was beginning to recover and lift its head again. I wrote up the old Cape Leforce legend in rhyme and sent it down home to the *Patriot*, no more of the *Examiner* for me!

Four weeks passed. One afternoon Father came in with a copy of the *Patriot*. My verses were in it! It was the first sweet bubble on the cup of success and of course it intoxicated me. There were some fearful printers' errors in the poem which fairly made the flesh creep on my bones, but it was my poem, and in a real newspaper! The moment we see our first darling brainchild arrayed in black type is never to be forgotten. It has in it some of the wonderful awe and delight that comes to a mother when she looks for the first time on the face of her first born.

During that winter I had other verses and articles printed. A story I had written in a prize competition was published in the Montreal *Witness*, and a descriptive article on Saskatchewan was printed in the Prince Albert *Times*, and copied and commented on favourably by several Winnipeg papers. After several effusions on "June" and kindred subjects appeared in that long-suffering *Patriot*, I was beginning to plume myself on being quite a literary person.

But the demon of filthy lucre was creeping into my heart. I wrote a story and sent it to the New York *Sun*, because I had been told that it paid for articles; and the New York *Sun* sent it back to me. I flinched, as from a slap in the face, but went on writing. You see I had learned the first, last, and middle lesson—"Never give up!"

The next summer I returned to Prince Edward Island and spent the following winter in Park Corner, giving music lessons and writing verses for the *Patriot*. Then I attended the Cavendish school for another year, studying for the Entrance Examination into Prince of Wales College. In the fall of 1803 I went to Charlottetown, and attended the Prince of Wales College that winter studying for a teacher's license.

I was still sending away things and getting them back. But one day I went into the Charlottetown post office and got a thin letter with the address of an American magazine in the corner. In it was a brief note accepting a poem, "Only a Violet." The editor offered me two subscriptions to the magazine in payment. I kept one myself and gave the other to a friend, and those magazines, with their vapid little stories, were the first tangible recompense my pen brought me.

"It is a start, and I mean to keep on," I find written in my old journal of that year. "Oh, I wonder if I shall ever be able to do anything worth while in the way of writing. It is my dearest ambition."

After leaving Prince of Wales College I taught school for a year in Bideford, Prince Edward Island. I wrote a good deal and learned a good deal, but still my stuff came back, except from two periodicals the editors of which evidently thought that literature was its own reward, and quite independent of monetary considerations. I often wonder that I did not give up in utter discouragement. At first I used to feel dreadfully hurt when a story or poem over which I had laboured and agonized came back, with one of those icy little rejection slips. Tears of disappointment *would* come in spite of myself, as I crept away to hide the poor, crimpled manuscript in the depths of my trunk. But after a while I got hardened to it and did not mind. I only set my teeth and said "I will succeed." I believed in myself and I struggled on alone, in secrecy and silence. I never told my ambitions and efforts and failures to anyone. Down, deep down, under all discouragement and rebuff, I knew I would "arrive" some day.

In the autumn of 1895 I went to Halifax and spent the winter taking a selected course in English literature at Dalhousie College. Through the winter came a "Big Week" for me. On Monday I received a letter from Golden Days, a Philadelphia juvenile, accepting a short story I had sent there and enclosing a cheque for five dollars. It was the first money my pen had ever earned; I did not squander it in riotous living, neither did I invest it in necessary boots and gloves. I went up town and bought five volumes of poetry with it—Tennyson, Byron, Milton, Longfellow, Whittier. I wanted something I could keep for ever in memory of having" arrived."

On Wednesday of the same week I won the prize of five dollars offered by the Halifax *Evening Mail* for the best letter on the subject, "Which has the greater patience—man or woman?"

My letter was in the form of some verses, which I had composed during a sleepless night and got up at three o'clock in the wee sma' hours to write down. On Saturday the *Youth's Companion* sent me a cheque for twelve dollars for a poem. I really felt quite bloated with so much wealth. Never in my life, before or since have I been so rich!

After my Dalhousie winter I taught school for two more years. In those two years I wrote scores of stories, generally for Sunday School publications and juvenile periodicals. The following entry from my journal refers to this period:

> I have grubbed away industriously all this summer and ground out stories and verses on days so hot that I feared my very marrow would melt and my gray matter be hopelessly sizzled up. But oh, I love my work! I love spinning stories, and I love to sit by the window of my room and shape some 'airy fairy' fancy into verse. I have got on well this summer and added several new journals to my list. They are a varied assortment, and their separate tastes all have to be catered to. I write a great many juvenile stories. I like doing these, but I should like it better if I didn't have to drag a 'moral' into most of them. They won't sell without it, as a rule. So in the moral must go, broad or subtle, as suits the fibre of the particular editor I have in view. The kind of juvenile story I like best to write—and read, too, for the matter of that—is a good, jolly one, "art for art's sake," or rather "fun for fun's sake," with no insidious moral hidden away in it like a pill in a spoonful of jam!

It was not always hot weather when I was writing. During one of those winters of school teaching I boarded in a very cold farmhouse. In the evenings, after a day of strenuous school work, I would be too tired to write. So I religiously arose an hour earlier in the mornings for that purpose. For five months I got up at six o'clock and dressed by lamplight. The fires would not yet be on, of course, and the house would be very cold. But I would put on a heavy coat, sit on my feet to keep them from freezing and with fingers so cramped that I could scarcely hold the pen, I would write my "stunt" for the day. Sometimes it would be a poem in which I would carol blithely of blue skies and rippling brooks and flowery meads! Then I would thaw out my hands, eat breakfast and go to school.

When people say to me, as they occasionally do, "Oh, how I envy you your gift, how I wish I could write as you do," I am inclined to wonder, with some inward amusement, how much they would have envied me on those dark, cold, winter mornings of my apprenticeship.

✿ Chapter Seven ✿

GRANDFATHER DIED IN 1898 and Grandmother was left alone in the old homestead. So I gave up teaching and stayed home with her. By 1901 I was beginning to make a "livable" income for myself by my pen, though that did not mean everything I wrote was accepted on its first journey. Far from it. Nine out of ten manuscripts came back to me. But I sent them out over and over again, and eventually they found resting places. Another extract from my journal may serve as a sort of milestone to show how far I had travelled.

March 21, 1901

Munsey's came to-day with my poem "Comparisons" in it, illustrated. It really *looked* nice. I've been quite in luck of late, for several new and good magazines have opened their portals to this poor wandering sheepkin of thorny literary ways. I feel that I am improving and developing in regard to my verses. I suppose it would be strange if I did not, considering how hard I study and work. Every now and then I write a poem which serves as a sort of landmark to emphasize my progress. I know, by looking back, that I could not have written it six months, or a year, or four years ago, any more than I could have made a garment the material of which was still unwoven. I wrote two poems this week. A year ago, I could not have written them, but now they come easily and naturally. This encourages me to hope that in the future I may achieve something worth while. I never expect to be famous. I merely want to have a recognized place among good workers in my chosen profession. That, I honestly believe, is happiness, and the harder to win the sweeter and more lasting when won.

In the fall of 1901 I went again to Halifax and worked for the winter on the staff of the *Daily Echo*, the evening edition of the *Chronicle*. A series of extracts from my journal will tell the tale of that experience with sufficient fulness.

11 November, 1901

I am here alone in the office of the *Daily Echo*. The paper is gone to press and the extra proofs have not yet begun to come down. Overhead, in the composing room, they are rolling machines and making a diabolical noise. Outside of the window the engine exhaust is puffing furiously. In the inner office two reporters are having a wrangle. And here sit I—the *Echo* proof-reader and general handy-man. Quite a 'presto change' from last entry!

I'm a newspaper woman!

Sounds nice? Yes, and the reality is very nice, too. Being of the earth, it is earthy, and has its drawbacks. Life in a newspaper office isn't all 'beer and skittles' any more than anywhere else. But on the whole it is not a bad life at all! I rather like proof-reading, although it is tedious. The headlines and editorials are my worst thorns in the flesh. Headlines have a natural tendency to depravity, and the editor-in-chief has a ghastly habit of making puns over which I am apt to come to grief. In spite of all my care 'errors will creep in' and then there is the mischief to pay. When I have nightmares now they are of headlines wildly askew and editorials hopelessly hocussed, which an infuriated chief is flourishing in my face.

The paper goes to press at 2.30, but I have to stay till six to answer the 'phone, sign for wires, and read extra proofs.

On Saturdays the *Echo* has a lot of extra stuff, a page of 'society letters' among the rest. It usually falls to my lot to edit these. Can't say I fancy the job much, but the only thing I positively abhor is 'faking' a society letter. This is one of the tricks of newspaperdom. When a society letter fails to turn up from a certain place—say from Windsor—in due time, the news editor slaps a Windsor Weekly down before me and says blandly, 'fake up a society letter from that, Miss Montgomery.'
So poor Miss Montgomery goes meekly to work, and concocts an introductory paragraph or so about 'autumn leaves' and 'mellow days' and 'October frosts,' or any old stuff like that to suit the season. Then I go carefully over the columns of the weekly, clip out all the available personals and news items, about weddings, and engagements, and teas, etc., hash them up in epistolary style, forge the Windsor correspondent's nom de plume—and there's your society letter! I used to include funerals, too, but I found the news editor blue-pencilled them. Evidently funerals have no place in society.

Then I write a column or so of giddy paragraphs for Monday's *Echo*. I call it "Around the Tea-Table," and sign it "Cynthia."

My office is a back room looking out on a back yard in the middle of the block. I don't know that all the Haligonian washerwomen live around it, but certainly a good percentage of them must, for the yard is a network of lines from which sundry and divers garments are always streaming gaily to the breezes. On the ground and over the roof cats are prowling continually, and when they fight, the walls resound with their howls. Most of them are lank, starved-looking beasties enough, but there is one lovely gray fellow who basks on a window sill opposite me and looks so much like 'Daffy' that, when I look at him, I could squeeze out a homesick tear if I were not afraid that would wash a clean spot on my grimy face. This office is really the worst place for getting dirty I ever was in.

November 18, 1901

Have had a difficult time trying to arrange for enough spare minutes to do some writing. I could not write in the evenings, I was always too tired. Besides, I had to keep my buttons sewed on and my stockings darned. Then I reverted to my old practice, and tried getting up at six in the morning. But it did not work, as of yore. I could never get to bed as early as I could when I was a country 'schoolma'am' and I found it impossible to do without a certain amount of sleep.

There was only one alternative.

Hitherto, I had thought that undisturbed solitude was necessary that the fire of genius might burn and even the fire for pot-boiling. I must be alone, and the room must be quiet. I could never have even imagined that I could possibly write anything in a newspaper office, with rolls of proof shooting down every ten minutes, people coming and conversing, telephones ringing, and machines being thumped and dragged overhead. I would have laughed at the idea, yea, I would have laughed it to scorn. But the impossible has happened. I am of one mind with the Irishman who said you could get used to anything, even to being hanged!

All my spare time here I write, and not such bad stuff either, since the *Delineator*, the *Smart Set* and *Ainslies'* have taken some of it. I have grown accustomed to stopping in the middle of a paragraph to interview a prowling caller, and to pausing in full career after an elusive rhyme, to read a lot of proof, and snarled-up copy.

Saturday, December 8, 1901

Of late I've been Busy with a capital B. 'Tending to office work, writing pot-boilers, making Christmas presents, etc., mostly etc.
   One of the" etcs." is a job I heartily detest. It makes my soul cringe. It is bad enough to have your flesh cringe, but when it strikes into your soul it gets on your spiritual nerves terribly. We are giving all the firms who advertise with us a free "write-up" of their holiday goods, and I have to visit all the stores, interview the proprietors, and crystallize my information into two "sticks" of copy. From three to five every afternoon I potter around the business blocks until my nose is purple with the cold and my fingers numb from much scribbling of notes.

Wednesday, December 12, 1901

It is an ill wind that blows no good and my disagreeable assignment has blown me some. The other evening I went in to write up the Bon Marche, which sets up to be the millinery establishment of Halifax, and I found the proprietor very genial. He said he was delighted that the *Echo* had sent a lady, and by way of encouraging it not to weary in well doing he would send me up one of the new walking hats if I gave the Bon Marche a good write-up. I rather thought he was only joking, but sure enough, when the write-up came out yesterday, up came the hat, and a very pretty one it is too.

Thursday, December 20, 1901

All the odd jobs that go a-begging in this office are handed over to the present scribe. The very queerest one up to date came yesterday.

The compositors were setting up, for the weekly edition, a story called 'A Royal Betrothal,' taken from an English paper, and when about half through they lost the copy. Whereupon the news-editor requested me to go and write an 'end' for the story. At first I did not think I could. What was set up of the story was not enough to give me any insight into the solution of the plot. Moreover, my knowledge of royal love affairs is limited, and I have not been accustomed to write with flippant levity of kings and queens.

However, I fell to work and somehow got it done. Today it came out, and as yet nobody has guessed where the 'seam' comes in. If the original author ever beholds it, I wonder what he will think.

I may remark, in passing, that more than ten years afterward I came across a copy of the original story in an old scrapbook, and was much amused to discover that the author's development of the plot was about as different from mine as anything could possibly be.

Thursday, December 27th, 1901

Christmas is over. I had been rather dreading it, for I had been expecting to feel very much the stranger in a strange land. But, as usual, anticipation was discounted by realization. I had a very pleasant time although not, of course, so wildly exhilarating as to endanger life, limb or nerves, which was, no doubt, just as well.

I had a holiday, the first since coming here, and so was haunted all day by the impression that it was Sunday. I had dinner at the *Halifax* with B. and spent the afternoon with her. In the evening we went to the opera to see *The Little Minister*. It was good but not nearly so good as the book. I don't care for dramatized novels. They always jar on my preconceptions of the characters. Also, I had to write a criticism of the play and cast for the *Chronicle* and I dislike that very much.

Saturday, March 29, 1902

This week has been a miserable one of rain and fog and neuralgia. But I've lived through it. I've read proofs and dissected headlines and fought with compositors and bandied jokes with the marine editor. I have ground out various blameless rhymes for a consideration of filthy lucre, and I've written one real poem out of my heart.

I hate my "pot-boiling" stuff. But it gives me the keenest pleasure to write something that is good, a fit and proper incarnation of the art I worship. The news-editor has just been in to give me an assignment for to-morrow, bad 'cess to him. It is Easter Sunday, and I have to write up the 'parade' down Pleasant Street after church, for Monday's *Echo*.

Palmday, May 3, 1902

I spent the afternoon" expurgating" a novel for the news-editor's use and behoof. When he was away on his vacation his substitute began to run a serial in the *Echo* called "Under the Shadow." Instead of getting some A.P.A. stuff as he should have done, he simply bought a sensational novel and used it. It was very long and was only about half done when the news-editor returned. So, as it would run all summer, in its present form, I was bidden to take it and cut mercilessly out all unnecessary stuff. I have followed instructions, cutting out most of the kisses and embraces, two-thirds of the love-making, and all the descriptions, with the happy result that I have reduced it to about a third of its normal length, and all I can say 'Lord, have mercy on the soul of the compositor who has set it up in its present mutilated condition.'

Saturday, May 31, 1901

I had a good internal laugh to-night. I was in a street car and two ladies beside me were discussing the serial that had just ended in the *Echo*. 'You know,' said one, 'it was the strangest story I ever read. It wandered on, chapter after chapter, for weeks, and never seemed to get anywhere; and then it just finished up in eight chapters, *licketty-split*. I can't understand it!'

I could have solved the mystery, but I didn't.

❧ Chapter Eight ❧

IN JUNE, 1902, I returned to Cavendish, where I remained unbrokenly for the next nine years. For the first two years after my return I wrote only short stories and serials as before. But I was beginning to think of writing a book. It had always been my hope and ambition to write one. But I never seemed able to make a beginning.

I have always hated beginning a story. When I get the first paragraph written I feel as though it were half done. The rest comes easily. To begin a book, therefore, seemed quite a stupendous task. Besides, I did not see just how I could get time for it. I could not afford to take the time from my regular writing hours. And, in the end, I never deliberately sat down and said "Go to! Here are pens, paper, ink and plot. Let me write a book. It really all just "happened."

I had always kept a notebook in which I jotted down, as they occurred to me, ideas for plots, incidents, characters, and descriptions. In the spring of 1904 I was looking over this notebook in search of some idea for a short serial I wanted to write for a certain Sunday School paper. I found a faded entry, written many years before: "Elderly couple apply to orphan asylum for a boy. By mistake a girl is sent them." I thought this would do. I began to block out the chapters, devise, and select incidents and "brood up" my heroine. Anne—she was not so named of malice aforethought, but flashed into my fancy already christened, even to the all important "e"—began to expand in such a fashion that she soon seemed very real to me and took possession of me to an unusual extent. She appealed to me, and I thought it rather a shame to waste her on an ephemeral little serial. Then the thought came, "Write a book. You have the central idea. All you need do is to spread it out over enough chapters to amount to a book."

The result was *Anne of Green Gables*. I wrote it in the evenings after my regular day's work was done, wrote most of it at the window of the little gable room which had been mine for many years. I began it, as I have said, in the spring of 1904. I finished it in the October of 1905.

Ever since my first book was published I have been persecuted by the question "Was so-and-so the original of such-and-such in your book?" And behind my back they don't put it in the interrogative form, but in the affirmative. I know many people who have asserted that they are well acquainted with the "originals" of my characters. Now, for my own part, I have never, during all the years I have studied human nature, met one human being who could, as a whole, be put into a book without injuring it. Any artist knows that to paint *exactly* from life is to give a false impression of the subject. *Study* from life he must, copying suitable heads or arms, appropriating bits of character, personal or mental idiosyncrasies, "making use of the real to perfect the ideal."

But the ideal, his ideal, must be behind and beyond it all. The writer must *create* his characters, or they will not be life-like.

With but one exception I have never drawn any of my book people from life. That exception was "Peg Bowen" in *The Story Girl*. And even then I painted the lily very freely. I have used real places in my books and many real incidents. But hitherto

I have depended wholly on the creative power of my own imagination for my characters.

Cavendish was "Avonlea" to a certain extent. "Lover's Lane" was a very beautiful lane through the woods on a neighbour's farm. It was a beloved haunt of mine from my earliest days. The "Shore Road" has a real existence, between Cavendish and Rustico. But the "White Way of Delight," "Wiltonmere," and "Violet Vale" were transplanted from the estates of my castles in Spain. "The Lake of Shining Waters" is generally supposed to be Cavendish Pond. This is not so. The pond I had in mind is the one at Park Corner, below Uncle John Campbell's house. But I suppose that a good many of the effects of light and shadow I had seen on the Cavendish pond figured unconsciously in my descriptions. Anne's habit of naming places was an old one of my own. I named all the pretty nooks and corners about the old farm. I had, I remember, a "Fairyland," a "Dreamland," a "Pussy-Willow Palace," a "No-Man's-Land," a "Queen's Bower," and many others. The "Dryads Bubble" was purely imaginary, but the "Old Log Bridge" was a real thing. It was formed by a single large tree that had blown down and lay across the brook. It had served as a bridge to the generation before my time, and was hollowed out like a shell by the tread of hundreds of passing feet. Earth had blown into the crevices, and ferns and grasses had found root and fringed it luxuriantly. Velvet moss covered its sides and below was a deep, clear, sun-flecked stream.

Anne's Katie Maurice was mine. In our sitting-room there had always stood a big bookcase used as a china cabinet. In each door was a large oval glass, dimly reflecting the room. When I was very small each of my reflections in these glass doors were "real folk" to my imagination. The one in the left-hand door was Katie Maurice, the one in the right, Lucy Gray. Why I named them thus I cannot say. Wordsworth's ballad had no connection with the latter, for I had never read it at that time. Indeed, I have no recollection of deliberately naming them at all. As far back as consciousness runs, Katie Maurice and Lucy Gray lived in the fairy room behind the bookcase. Katie Maurice was a little girl like myself, and I loved her dearly. I would stand before that door and prattle to Katie for hours, giving and receiving confidences. In especial, I liked to do this at twilight, when the fire had been lit and the room and its reflections were a glamour of light and shadow.

Lucy Gray was grown-up and a widow! I did not like her as well as Katie. She was always sad, and always had dismal stories of her troubles to relate to me; nevertheless, I visited her scrupulously in turn, lest her feelings should be hurt, because she was jealous of Katie, who also disliked her. All this sounds like the veriest nonsense, but I cannot describe how real it was to me. I never passed through the room without a wave of my hand to Katie in the glass door at the other end.

The notable incident of the liniment cake happened when I was teaching school in Bideford and boarding at the Methodist parsonage there. Its charming mistress flavoured a layer cake with anodyne liniment one day. Never shall I forget the taste of that cake and the fun we had over it, for the mistake was not discovered until tea-time. A strange minister was there to tea that night. He ate every crumb of his piece of cake. What he thought of it we never discovered. Possibly he imagined it was simply some new-fangled flavouring.

Many people have told me that they regretted Matthew's death in *Green Gables*. I regret it myself. If I had the book to write over again I would spare Matthew for several years. But when I wrote it I thought he must die, that there might be a necessity for self-sacrifice on Anne's part, so poor Matthew joined the long procession of ghosts that haunt my literary past.

Well, my book was finally written. The next thing was to find a publisher. I typewrote it myself, on my old second-hand typewriter that never made the capitals plain and wouldn't print "w" at all, and I sent it to a new American firm that had recently come to the front with several "best sellers." I thought I might stand a better chance with a new firm than with an old established one that had already a preferred list of writers. But the new firm very promptly sent it back. Next I sent it to one of the "old, established firms," and the old established firm sent it back. Then I sent it, in turn, to three "Betwixt-and-between firms," and they all sent it back. Four of them returned it with a cold, printed note of rejection; one of them "damned with faint praise." They wrote that "Our readers report that they find some merit in your story, but not enough to warrant its acceptance."

That finished me. I put *Anne* away in an old hat-box in the clothes room, resolving that some day when I had time I would take her and reduce her to the original seven chapters of her first incarnation. In that case I was tolerably sure of getting thirty-five dollars for her at least, and perhaps even forty.

The manuscript lay in the hatbox until I came across it one winter day while rummaging. I began turning over the leaves, reading a bit here and there. It didn't seem so very bad. "I'll try once more," I thought. The result was that a couple of months later an entry appeared in my journal to the effect that my book had been accepted. After some natural jubilation I wrote: "The book mayor may not succeed. I wrote it for love, not money, but very often such books are the most successful, just as everything in the world that is born of true love has life in it, as nothing constructed for mercenary ends can ever have.

"Well, I've written my book! The dream dreamed years ago at that old brown desk in school has come true at last after years of toil and struggle. And the realization is sweet, almost as sweet as the dream."

When I wrote of the book succeeding or not succeeding, I had in mind only a very moderate success indeed, compared to that which it did attain. I never dreamed that it would appeal to young and old. I thought girls in their teens might like to read it, that was the only audience I hoped to reach. But men and women who are grandparents have written to tell me how they loved *Anne*, and boys at college have done the same. The very day on which these words are written has come a letter to me from an English lad of nineteen, totally unknown to me, who writes that he is leaving for "the front" and wants to tell me "before he goes" how much my books and especially *Anne* have meant to him. It is in such letters that a writer finds meet reward for all sacrifice and labor.

Well, *Anne* was accepted; but I had to wait yet another year before the book was published. Then on June 20th, 1908, I wrote in my journal:

"To-day has been, as Anne herself would say, 'an epoch in my life.' My book came to-day, 'spleet-new' from the publishers. I candidly confess that it was to me a proud and wonderful and thrilling moment. There, in my hand, lay the material realization of all the dreams and hopes and ambitions and struggles of my whole conscious existence—my first book. Not a great book, but mine, mine, mine, something which I had created."

I have received hundreds of letters from all over the world about *Anne*. Some odd dozen of them were addressed, not to me, but to "Miss Anne Shirley, Green Gables, Avonlea, Prince Edward Island." They were written by little girls who had such a touching faith in the real flesh and blood existence of Anne that I always hated to destroy it. Some of my letters were decidedly amusing. One began impressingly, "My dear long-lost uncle," and the writer went on to claim me as Uncle Lionel, who seemed to have disappeared years ago. She wound up by entreating me to write to my "affectionate niece" and explain the reason of my long silence. Several people wrote me that their lives would make very interesting stories, and if I would write them and give them half the proceeds they would give me "the facts!" I answered only one of these letters, that of a young man who had enclosed stamps for a reply. In order to let him down as gently as possible, I told him that I was not in any need of material, as I had books already planned out which would require at least ten years to write. He wrote back that he had a great deal of patience and would cheerfully wait until ten years had expired; then he would write again. So, if my own invention gives out, I can always fall back on what that young man assured me was "a thrilling life-history!"

Green Gables has been translated into Swedish and Dutch. My copy of the Swedish edition always gives me the inestimable boon of a laugh. The cover design is a full length figure of Anne, wearing a sunbonnet, carrying the famous carpetbag, and with hair that is literally of an intense scarlet!

With the publication of *Green Gables* my struggle was over. I have published six novels since then. *Anne of Avonlea* came out in 1909, followed in 1910 by *Kilmeny of the Orchard*. This latter story was really written several years before *Green Gables*, and ran as a serial in an American magazine, under another title. Therefore some sage reviewers amused me not a little by saying that the book showed "the insidious influence of popularity and success" in its style and plot!

The Story Girl was written in 1910 and published in 1911. It was the last book I wrote in my old home by the gable window where I had spent so many happy hours of creation. It is my own favourite among my books, the one that gave me the greatest pleasure to write, the one whose characters and landscape seem to me most real. All the children in the book are purely imaginary. The old "King Orchard" was a compound of our old orchard in Cavendish and the orchard at Park Corner. "Peg Bowen" was suggested by a half-witted, gypsy-like personage who roamed at large for many years over the Island and was the terror of my childhood. We children were always being threatened that if we were not good Peg would catch us. The threat did not make us good, it only made us miserable.

Poor Peg was really very harmless, when she was not teased or annoyed. If she were, she could be vicious and revengeful enough. In winter she lived in a little hut in the woods, but as soon as the spring came the lure of the open road proved too much for her, and she started on a tramp which lasted until the return of winter snows. She was known over most of the Island. She went bareheaded and barefooted, smoked a pipe, and told extraordinary tales of her adventures in various places. Occasionally she would come to church, stalking unconcernedly up the aisle to a prominent seat. She never put on hat or shoes on such occasions, but when she wanted to be especially grand she powdered face, arms and legs with *flour*!

As I have already said, the story of Nancy and Betty Sherman was founded on fact. The story of the captain of the *Fanny* is also literally true. The heroine is still living, or was a few years ago, and still retains much of the beauty which won the Captain's heart. "The Blue Chest of Rachel Ward" was another "ower-true tale." Rachel Ward was Eliza Montgomery, a cousin of my father's, who died in Toronto a few years ago. The blue chest was in the kitchen of Uncle John Campbell's house at Park Corner from 1849 until her death. We children heard its story many a time and speculated and dreamed over its contents, as we sat on it to study our lessons or eat our bed-time snacks.

❦ Chapter Nine ❧

IN THE WINTER of 1911 , Grandmother Macneill died at the age of eighty-seven, and the old home was broken up. I stayed at Park Corner until July; and on July 5th was married. Two days later my husband and I sailed from Montreal on the *Megantic* for a trip through the British Isles, another "dream come true," for I had always wished to visit the old land of my forefathers. A few extracts from the journal of my trip, may be of interest.

Glasgow, July 20, 1912

Thursday afternoon we left for an excursion to Oban, Staffa, and Iona. We went by rail to Oban and the scenery was very beautiful, especially along Loch Awe, with its ruined castle. Beautiful, yes! And yet neither there nor elsewhere in England or Scotland, did I behold a scene more beautiful than can be seen any evening at home, standing on the "old church hill" and looking afar over New London Harbor. But then—we have no ruined castles there, nor the centuries of romance they stand for!

Oban is a picturesque little town, a fringe of houses built along the shore of a land-locked harbour, with wooded mountains rising steeply behind them. Next morning we took the boat to Iona. It was a typical, Scottish day, bright and sunny one hour, showery or misty the next. For a few hours I enjoyed the sail very much. The wild, rugged scenery of cape and bay and island and bleak mountain—the whole of course, peppered with ruined, ivy-hung castles—was an ever changing panorama of interest, peopled with the shades of the past.

Then, too, we had a Cook's party of French tourists on board. They jabbered incessantly. There was one nice old fellow in particular, with a pleasant, bronzed face and twinkling black eyes, who seemed to be the expounder-in-chief of the party. They got into repeated discussions, and when the arguments reached a certain pitch of intensity, he would spring to his feet, confront the party, wave his arms, umbrella, and guide book wildly in the air, and lay down the law in a most authoritative tone and fashion.

As the forenoon wore away I began to lose interest in everything. Ruined castle, towering mountain, white torrent, ghosts, and French tourists lost their charm. In the morning I had been much worried because I heard that it might be too rough to stop at Staffa, and I wanted so badly to see Fingal's Cave. But now I did not care in the least for Fingal's Cave, or for any other earthly thing. For the first time in my life I was horribly seasick.

The steamer did stop at Staffa, however, and two boatloads went ashore. I let them go. What cared I? The waves would not have daunted me, the pouring rain would not have appalled me, but seasickness!

However, the steamer was now still and I began to feel better. By the time the boats came back for the second load I was quite well and once more it seemed a thing of first importance to see Fingal's Cave. I joyfully scrambled down into the boat and was rowed ashore with the others to the Clamshell cave.

From there we had to scramble over what seemed an interminably long distance—but really I suppose it was nor more than a quarter of a mile—over the wet, slippery, basalt columns that fringe the shore, hanging in the worst places to a rope strung along the cliff. Owing to my much scrambling over the rocks of Cavendish shore in early life, I got on very well and even extorted a compliment from the dour guide; but some of the tourists slipped to an alarming degree. Never shall I forget the yelps and sprawls of the old Frenchman aforesaid.

Nobody fell off, however, and eventually we found ourselves in Fingal's Cave, and felt repaid for all our exertions.

'Tis a most wonderful and majestic place, like an immense Gothic cathedral. It is hard to believe that it could have been fashioned merely by a freak of nature. I think everyone there felt awed; even those irrepressible French tourists were silent for a little time. As I stood there and listened to the deep, solemn echo of the waves the memory of a verse of Scripture came to me "He inhabiteth the halls of eternity." And it seemed to me that I stood in very truth in a temple of the Almighty that had not been builded by hands.

We went on to lona and landed there for a brief, hurried, scrambling exploration. lona is interesting as the scene of St. Columba's ministry. His ancient cathedral is still there. Of greater interest to me was the burial place of the earliest Scottish kings, about sixty of them, it is said, finishing with that Duncan who was murdered by Macbeth. They were buried very simply, those warriors of ancient days. There they lie, in their island cemetery, beneath the gray sky. Neither "storied urn nor animated bust" mark their resting place. Each grave is covered simply by a slab of worn, carved stone. But they sleep none the less soundly for that, lulled by the eternal murmur of the waves around them.

I would have liked to have spent several days in Iona, prowling by myself around its haunted ruins and getting acquainted with its quaint inhabitants. There is really little pleasure in a hurried scramble around such places in the midst of a chattering, exclaiming mob of tourists. For me, at least, solitude is necessary to real enjoyment of such places. I must be alone, or with a few 'kindred souls' before I can dream and muse, and bring back to life the men and women who once dwelt there and made the places famous.

We returned to Glasgow yesterday by water and were glutted with scenery. I was very tired when we reached our hotel. But weariness fell away from me when I found letters from home. How good they tasted in a foreign land! They bridged the gulf of ocean, and I saw the Cavendish hills and the green gloom of the maple wood at Park Corner. Ah! beautiful as the old world is, the homeland is the best.

July 30, 1912
Royal Hotel,
Prince's St.,
Edinburgh

Monday we went out to Ayr with a Cook guide. As a rule we dislike the Cook parties and go alone wherever we can. But this expedition was pleasant, as there were only two besides ourselves and they were Canadians, Mr. and Mrs. T. from Ontario. We had also a very nice guide. Two things subtracted from the pleasure of the day, it poured rain most of the time and I had a grumbling facial neuralgia. But in spite of both drawbacks I enjoyed myself 'where'er we trod 'twas haunted, holy ground.'

We saw the room—the low-ceilinged, humble little room where once a cotter's son was 'royal born by right divine,' and we explored the ruins of the old Alloway Kirk made classic forever by Tam O'Shanter's adventures.

Then we went to the Burns monument just because it was on the list of 'sights' and the guide was bound to do his duty by us. I have no interest whatever in monuments. They bore me horribly. But two things in the monument did interest me, a lock of Highland Mary's fair hair and the Bible upon which she and Burns swore their troth in their parting tryst. Poor, sweet Highland Mary! I don't suppose she was anything more than a winsome little country lass, no sweeter or prettier than thousands of other maidens who have lived and died, if not unwept, at least unhonoured and unsung. But a great genius flung over her the halo of his love and lo! she is one of the immortals, one of the fair ladies of old romance who will be forever remembered because of the man who loved her. She is of the company of Laura and Beatrice, and Stella, of Lucasta and Julia, and of the unknown lady of Arvers' sonnet.

Wednesday we went to the Trossachs. This is one of the expeditions I have looked forward to all my life, ever since I read "The Lady of the Lake" in schooldays. Sitting behind my old desk at school I dreamed out the panorama of hill and lake and pass, where Ellen lived and Fitz-James wandered and Roderick Dhu brooded like a storm cloud over a Highland hill. And I made a covenant with myself that when my ship came in I should go and see it.

We sailed up Loch Lomond to Inversnaid and there took coaches for a five-mile drive across to Loch Katrine. Of all the ways of locomotion I have ever tried I like coaching best. It beats motoring 'hollow.' We soon reached Stronachlachar, which in spite of its dreadful name, is an exquisite spot, and took the boat down Loch Katrine to the Trossachs pier.

I cannot decide whether Loch Katrine disappointed me or not. I think it did, a little. It was as beautiful as I had dreamed it, but it was not *my* Loch Katrine, not quite the Loch Katrine of my "Chateau en Espagne." And I resented the difference, as one might resent a change made in his childhood's home on going back to it after long years.

The lower portion of the lake is certainly much smaller than my idea of it as given by the poem. And the famous 'Silver Strand' is a poor affair now. Since the instalment of the Glasgow waterworks the lake has risen several feet and covered 'the beach of pebbles white as snow.' I brought a handful of them home with me as souvenirs. But I think I shall keep the Loch Katrine of my dream in my geography of the "Lady of the Lake." I like it better than the real one.

We coached through the Trossachs to the Trossachs hotel. The Trossachs is beautiful and grand and perhaps before the carriage road was made it was wild enough, especially for some benighted wanderer who had all too good reason to fear "Highland plunderers." But it is far from being the wild, riven, precipitous dell of my fancy. No, it is not the Trossachs where I have so often wandered with Fitz-James.

The hotel is in a lovely spot, on the shore of Loch Achray.

"Where shall we find in foreign land
So lone a lake, so sweet a strand?"

Yet Loch Achray, too, was on a smaller scale than I had expected. We walked along it that night as far as the 'Brig of Turk,' gathering bell-heather and bluebells as we went.

Scottish bluebells are certainly the sweetest things! They seem the very incarnation of old Scotia's romance.

Next morning we walked through the Trossachs to Loch Katrine in a pouring rain and hired one of the boatmen to row us to and around "Ellen's Isle." I don't think I liked it because it, too, was not the islet of my dream, and I was conscious of a foolish disappointment.

Ben Venue, however, did not disappoint me. It dominates the landscape. Everywhere we went, there was old Ben Venue, rugged and massive, with a cloud-wreath resting on his 'summit hoar.' I was very sorry that the night we spent there was wet. I should have loved to have seen a sunset effect on Ben Venue.

August 6, 1912

Last Monday morning we went by train to Melrose and coached over six miles of most beautiful road to Abbotsford. Although we went on our own account we could not help falling in with a Cook excursion and this somewhat spoiled the day for us. But the scenery along the road is exquisite and we saw the Eildon Hills, cleft in three by the spells of wizardry. Abbotsford is most interesting, crowded with relics I should have loved to have dreamed over in solitude. But that might not be. The rooms were filled by a chattering crowd, harangued by a glib guide. I wondered if Scott would have liked to think of his home being so over-run by a horde of curious sight-seers.

We drove from Abbotsford to Dryburgh where Scott is buried. As we were able to escape from the "Cookies" here we enjoyed the magnificent ruin doubly. Then we returned to Melrose and explored the ruins of the Abbey there. We could not follow Scott's advice, which I never believed he failed, as is asserted, to take himself, and view it by moonlight. But in that mellow, golden-gray evening light it was beautiful enough, beautiful and sad, with the little bluebells growing in its ruined courts and over its old graves. Michael Scott is reputed to be buried there, and there the heart of Robert Bruce was buried, and doubtless, rests as quietly as though it had, according to his wish, been laid in the soil of the Holy Land.

There is some wonderful hand-carving still left in Melrose, and the little hand high up on one of the arches is as sugges-tive as it is beautiful. What fair lady's hand was chiselled there in lasting stone? One cannot but think it was wrought by a lover. On Wednesday we left for Inverness, but stopped off *en route* to visit Kirriemuir, the "Thrums" of Barrie's stories. In particular, I wanted to see the 'Den' where Sentimental Tommy and his cronies held their delightful revels. It is a love-ly spot. One thing about it made me feel at home, its paths, which Barrie calls 'pink,' are the very red of our own island roads. I could have fancied that I was prowling in the woods around Lovers' Lane.

✦ Chapter Ten ✦

O F ALL THE places we have visited in Scotland thus far I like Inverness best. In itself it is only a small gray town but the surrounding scenery is magnificent.

We drove out to Culloden the evening of our arrival and it is one of the drives that, for sheer pleasure, will always stand out in my memory. The road was exceedingly lovely and we were fortunate enough to have a nice old driver who knew all the history and legend of everything, and was very willing to tell it in delightful broad Scotch.

The next day we visited Tomnahurich, the famous cemetery of Inverness. It deserves its fame; I am sure it must be the most beautiful cemetery in the world. It is a large hill outside the city, rising in a perfect cone, and thickly covered with trees. The name is a Gaelic word meaning 'the hill of the fairies,' and surely it must once have been a spot meet for a fairy kingdom and the revels of Titania. Seen at eventide, against a sunset sky, it seems a veritable outpost of the Land of Old Romance.

We returned by way of the Caledonian Canal to Fort William, and thence by train. The sunset effects on the mountains along our way were wonderful. If I were to live near mountains for any length of time I should learn to love them *almost* as much as I love the sea.

August 13, 1912
Last Monday we visited Roslin Chapel, a wonderful specimen

of Gothic work in perfect preservation. This is the chapel of Scott's ballad, "Fair Rosabelle":

> "Seemed all on fire that chapel proud
> Where Roslin's chiefs uncoffined lie."

Wednesday we left Edinburgh and went to Alloa to visit friends. Thursday we 'did' Dollar Glen. I had never heard of this place until Mr. M. of Alloa told us of it, yet it is one of the wildest, grandest spots we have seen in all Scotland. If Scott had touched it with his genius it would be as widely known as the Trossachs. Indeed, it is much what I had imagined the Trossachs to be. Dollar Glen is like a deep gash cleft down through the heart of the mountain.

Stirling and Abbey Craig on Friday, places steeped with romance. Yesterday we came to Berwick to spend a week in the Marmion country. Mr. M. and Miss A. came with us. Berwick is a most quaint, antiquated old town. As we live on the Spittal side, when we want to go anywhere we have to be rowed over the river mouth by one of the half-dozen quaint old ferrymen who have boats for hire. Last night we all went for a walk along the Spittal shore by moonlight. It was beautiful but so like the Cavendish shore that it made me bitterly homesick.

Carlisle, August 20

We are spending Sunday in Carlisle perforce, since we could not get any farther last night, owing to the big railway strike which has been paralysing Britain this past week. At Berwick we did not suffer from it, nor heed it. We let the outer world go by and lived in realms of romance where ferry boats and shank's mare were the only desired means of locomotion.

Last Monday we went to Holy Island and explored the ruins of the old Abbey which was the scene of Constance de Beverley's death in *Marmion*. We had an enjoyable sail down to Holy Island but the return home was sadly different. It was quite rough and how that wretched little steamer pitched and rolled! Both our gentlemen became so overcome that they had to retire temporarily from the scene, while Miss A. and I fought off surrender only by a tremendous effort of will and would have suffered less I think if we had just allowed ourselves to go!

Luckily seasickness is never fatal and next day we were all ready for an excursion to Norham Castle, a very ruinous ruin.

Growing all over the grounds was a little blue flower which I never saw anywhere else save in the front orchard of the old home in Cavendish. Great-grandmother Woolner had brought it out from England with her. It gave me an odd feeling of pain and pleasure mingled, to find it growing there around that old ruined Scottish castle which seemed to belong so utterly to another time and another order of things. We walked from Norham to Ladykirk and then back by the Tweed. When we grew tired we sat down on its bank and dreamed dreams. What meeter place could there be for dreaming than the twilit banks of Tweed?

Next day we went to Flodden Field. It disappointed me unreasonably, it was all so peaceful, and harvest-hued, and agricultural. I felt as aggrieved as though I had had any right to expect to see a mediaeval battle being fought under my eyes.

Thursday afternoon we had a delightful little expedition to Homecliffe Glen and its deserted old mill. It might serve as a scene for a ghost story. In the midst of the ravine we came upon a clump of spruce trees literally loaded with gum, the first I had seen since leaving home. Spruce gum and the delights of picking it seem quite unknown in Scotland. We spent a half-hour picking it. To me and my husband the gum tasted delicious, but neither Mr. M. nor Miss A. liked its flavor declaring it was 'bitter.'

York, England
August 27, 1912
Last Monday we went to Keswick and stayed there until Thursday. It is impossible to exaggerate the beauty of the Lake District:

> "The haughtiest heart its wish might bound
> Through life to dwell delighted here."

And then it is so interwoven with much of the best in English literature. The very spirit of Wordsworth seems to haunt those enchanted valleys, those wild passes, those fairy-like lakes.

Monday afternoon we took a coach-drive around Lake Derwentwater. All was beautiful. An interesting sight was the Castle Rock, which figures as the magic castle of St. John in Scott's "Bridal of Triermain." There is only one point where the resemblance to a castle—said to be very striking—can be seen, and we were not fortunate enough to see it from that particular point.

Tuesday we went to Buttermere Lake; Wednesday we motored for eighty miles around Lake Windermere. Some of the huge rocks on the mountain tops are of very peculiar shape. One of them is named, 'The Lady Playing on the Organ.' It is on the very top of a majestic mountain and certainly does, from one point of view, look exactly like a woman seated at a huge organ. Somehow, it captivated my imagination and I wove a hundred fancies around it. Who was the player, sitting forever at her mighty instrument? And what wonderful melodies did she play on it when the winds of heaven blew about her and the mountain tempest thundered and the great stars stayed to listen?

That evening we walked out to the 'Druid Circle,' a ring of large stones on a hill-top, supposed to have been in old time a temple of the sun.

Nothing I have seen thus far made such a vivid impression on me as this. The situation is magnificent. The hill is completely encircled by a ring of the most famous mountains in the Lake District, Helvellyn and Skiddaw among them, and the sense of majesty produced was overwhelming. Certainly those old sun-worshippers knew how to choose their sites. To stand there, at sunset, in the temple of a departed creed, surrounded by that assembly of everlasting hills and picture the rites, perchance dark and bloody, which must once have been celebrated there, was an experience never to be forgotten.

Friday we came to York, mainly to see the magnificent cathedral. It *is* magnificent, a dream of beauty made lasting in stone.

Yesterday afternoon I became the proud and happy possessor of a pair of china dogs!

I have been pursuing china dogs all over England and Scotland. When I was a little girl, visiting at Grandfather Montgomery's I think the thing that most enthralled me was a pair of china dogs which always sat on the sitting room mantel. They were white with green spots all over them; and Father told me that whenever they heard the clock strike twelve at midnight they bounded down on the hearth-rug and barked. It was, therefore, the desire of my heart to stay up until twelve some night and witness this performance, and hard indeed did I think the hearts of my elders when this was denied me. Eventually I found out, I forget how, that the dogs did nothing of the sort. I was much disappointed over this but more grieved still over the discovery that Father had told me something that wasn't true. However, he restored my faith in him by pointing out that he had only said the dogs would jump down when they *heard* the clock strike. China dogs, of course, could not hear.

I have always hankered to possess a pair of similar dogs, and, as those had been purchased in London, I hoped when I came over here, I would find something like them. Accordingly I have haunted the antique shops in every place I have been but, until yesterday, without success. Dogs, to be sure, there were in plenty but not the dogs of my quest. There was an abundance of dogs with black spots and dogs with red spots; but nowhere the aristocratic dogs with green spots.

Yesterday in a little antique shop near the great Minster I found a pair of lovely dogs and snapped them up on the spot. To be sure they had no green spots. The race of dogs with green spots seems to have become extinct. But my pair have lovely gold spots and are much larger than the old Park Corner dogs. They are over a hundred years old and hope they will preside over my Lares and Penates with due dignity and aplomb.

Russell Hotel, London
September 18, 1912
So much has been crammed into this past fortnight that I have a rather overfed feeling mentally. But when time is limited and

sights unlimited what are harassed travellers to do? The British Museum, the Tower, Westminister Abbey, Crystal Palace, Kenilworth Castle, the Shakespeare Land, Hampton Court, Salisbury and Stonehenge, Windsor and Parks and Gardens galore!

Our hotel is in Russell Square, the haunt of so many of the characters in *Vanity Fair*. One expects to see Amelia peering out of a window looking for George, or perhaps Becky watching for Jos.

Our afternoon at Kenilworth Castle was a delight. Of course, we had to be pestered with a guide; but I succeeded in forgetting him, and roamed the byways of romance alone. I saw Kenilworth in its pride, when aspiring Leicester entertained haughty Elizabeth. I pictured poor Amy Robsart creeping humbly into the halls where she should have reigned as Mistress. Back they thronged from the past, those gay figures of olden days, living, loving, hating, plotting as of yore.

Last Thursday we went to see the Temple Church, in the grounds of which Oliver Goldsmith is buried. The church is a quaint old place, set in a leafy square which, despite the fact that Fleet Street is roaring just outside it, is as peaceful and silent as a Cavendish road. But when I recall that square it is not of the quaint old church and Poor Noll's grave that I shall think. No, it will be of a most charming and gentlemanly pussy cat, of exquisite manners, who came out of one of the houses and walked across the square to meet us. He was large and handsome and dignified, and anyone could see with half an eye that he belonged to the caste of Vere de Vere. He purred most mellifluously as I patted him, and rubbed himself against my boots as though we were old acquaintances, as perchance we were in some other incarnation. Nine out of ten cats would have insisted on accompanying us over to Oliver's grave, and perhaps been too hard to get rid of. Not so this Marquis of Carabas. He sat gravely down and waited until we had gone on, seen the grave and returned to where he sat. Then he stood up, received our farewell pats, waved his tail amiably, and walked gravely back to the door from which he had emerged, having done the honor of his demesne in most irreproachable fashion. Truly he did give the world assurance of a cat!

We sail for home next Thursday on the *Adriatic*. I am glad, for I am replete with sight-seeing. I want now to get back to Canada and gather my scattered household gods around me for a new consecration.

As my husband was pastor of an Ontario congregation, I had now to leave Prince Edward Island and move to Ontario. Since my marriage I have published four books, *Chronicles of Avonlea*, *The Golden Road*, *Anne of The Island*, and *The Watchman*, the latter being a volume of collected verse.

The "Alpine Path" has been climbed, after many years of toil and endeavor. It was not an easy ascent, but even in the struggle at its hardest there was a delight and a zest known only to those who aspire to the heights.

> "He ne'er is crowned
> With immortality, who fears to follow
> Where airy voices lead."

True, most true! We must follow our "airy voices," follow them through bitter suffering and discouragement and darkness, through doubt and disbelief, through valleys of humiliation and over delectable hills where sweet things would lure us from our quest, ever and always must we follow, if we would reach the "far-off divine event" and look out thence to the aerial spires of our City of Fulfilment.